MW00761699

Martin Lynch was born in 1950 in the Gilnahirk district of Belfast. One of the north of Ireland's most respected playwrights, his work for stage includes *The Interrogation of Ambrose Fogarty* (1982), *Minstrel Boys* (1985), *The Stone Chair* (1989), *Rinty* (1990) and *Pictures of Tomorrow* (1994). His most recent play is *The History of the Troubles According to Me Da* (2002). He has for many years been involved in the community drama movement and has been writer-in-residence at the Lyric Players' Theatre, Belfast, and the University of Ulster.

DOCKERS
& WELCOME TO BLADONMORE ROAD

DOCKERS
& WELCOME TO BLADONMORE ROAD

MARTIN LYNCH

LAGAN PRESS
BELFAST
2003

Published by
Lagan Press
138 University Avenue
Belfast BT7 1GZ

© Martin Lynch, 2003

The moral right of the author has been asserted.

ISBN: 1 873687 64 8

Author: Lynch, Martin
Title: Dockers
& Welcome to Bladonmore Road
2003

Front Cover: from the Lyric Players' Theatre production of *Dockers*
(courtesy of Alwyn James
and the Linen Hall Library)
Design: December Publications
Set in New Baskerville
Printed by Eastwood Printing, Belfast

CONTENTS

DOCKERS

Dockers was first performed at the Lyric Players' Theatre, Belfast, on 12th January 1981. It was directed by Sam McCready. The cast was as follows:

John Graham	Oliver Maguire
Theresa Graham	Stella McCusker
Buckets McGuinness	Louis Rolston
Leg McNamara	J.J. Murphy
Hughie McNamara	Ian McElhinney
Danny-boy McNamara	Peter Quigley
Jack Henry	George Shane
Harry McKibben	Mel Austin
Jimmy Sweeney	Mark Shelley
Sarah Montague	Leila Webster
Mary-Ann McKeown	Maureen Dow
Barney	Michael Gormley

The play is set in 1962. The location is the Sailortown district of Belfast.

ACT ONE

SCENE 1

The scene is an employment schooling-shed for dockworkers. It is desolated, barren and grey. Along the wall is a three-foot high wooden platform, protected by a steel crush barrier. A group of dockers enters casually, some engaged in conversation and some reading newspapers.

JOHN: I don't care. If you're drivin' that winch, Leg, you'll not get me down in the houl' of that boat.

LEG: I've never caused an accident in my life.

JOHN: It's not for the want of tryin'.

LEG: You ask your da who's the best winchman he ever saw.

JOHN: I'd believe you, but millions wouldn't.

[The dockers are standing beside or near the platform.]

LEG: Just ask your da.

[A docker enters, in a slight hurry.]

BUCKETS: Well, young Graham, what's goin'?

JOHN: Ach, Buckets, what about ye? Aye, there's a fair bit of work this mornin'. As far as I hear, the Ghent boat's in.

BUCKETS: Oh, give that a wide berth. What's Sweeney at?

[The foreman, JIMMY SWEENEY, enters with JACK HENRY, the union chairman. SWEENEY jumps up on the platform. HENRY exits.]

JOHN: Beg stuff.

BUCKETS: That's no good, either. What about your man?

JOHN: Fruit boat. But he's finished at twelve and has his own gang.

BUCKETS: Is Wicked Moustache out this mornin'?

JOHN: Aye, he's over there, but he's at beg stuff, too.

BUCKETS: In the name of Jasis, is there nothin' else? Every time I go near a beg boat, I'm bad with m'chest for days after it. Friggin' grain! No good for the drinkin', y'know.

JOHN [*mockingly*]: When was the last time you were at a beg boat?

BUCKETS: Who? What? I wisht I'd a pound in m'pocket for every beg boat I'd worked at down the years. What are you slabberin' about anyway? You're only a meal-hour round the dock. What? The likes of you givin' me bettins?

JOHN: I'm only havin' you on, Buckets. Here, away over there. The Headline has a handy wee Timber boat in.

BUCKETS: What da buck ... get away ... bucksake! Timber boats!

JOHN: I don't know why you got outta your bed a'tall this mornin'.

BUCKETS: Nor do I. I'm away up to the corner to wait on Barney's openin'. I'll see you later.

JOHN: Okay, Buckets, see ya. [BUCKETS *turns to go, then stops.*]

BUCKETS: By the way, young Graham, I hope you're not thinkin' I'm walkin' away from work. Not a'tall. I'm just givin' the non-union men a chance to get a day's work. [*He smiles.*]

JOHN: Get away of that with ye, Buckets. [BUCKETS *walks towards exit.* JOHN *shouts after him*] I'm gonna tell your oul' woman you didn't weigh in for work this mornin'!

BUCKETS: No, tell your own ma about the time your da lost his pay packet down the toilet in Dubarry's!

JOHN: At least my da earned a wage!

BUCKETS: Ya don't call me Shitey Pound Note!

JOHN: Ach, away on to hell of that with ye!

BUCKETS: Shitey Pound Note! [*He exits shouting*] Aye, tell your ma about the time your da lost his pay packet down the toilet in a brothel! Shitey Pound Note!

[JOHN GRAHAM *shakes his head and smiles.* JIMMY SWEENEY *speaks to a man standing directly below him.*]

SWEENEY: Are we ready to start, McKibben. It's after eight nigh!

MCKIBBEN: Wait and I'll go and see if there's anybody still comin' down the road.

[MCKIBBEN *walks up to the exit and looks into the distance. He turns back and shouts as he is half-way across.*]

MCKIBBEN: Alright! Away yiz go!

[*The men quickly bunch up against the crush barrier directly under* JIMMY SWEENEY. *The foreman, quite selectively, picks and chooses which men he is employing by handing each man a small disc. As a man is selected, he exits.*]

SWEENEY: Right, Kelly! You! O'Neill! You! McNamara! Quinn!

[MCKIBBEN *pushes his way forward to the front of the platform, by which time the remaining men are jostling each other, with arms outstretched.*]

MCKIBBEN: Come on, men! Stand back and give him a chance. Do yiz wanna make exhibitions of yourselves? Come on!

[MCKIBBEN *places himself directly below the foreman.*]

SWEENEY: McKibben! And Graham! That's it!

[SWEENEY *jumps down and quickly exits.* HUGHIE MCNAMARA *enters the shed as* JOHN GRAHAM *is about to exit.*]

HUGHIE: Nothin' left, John?

JOHN: Nope. You can see for yourself. There's forty or fifty first-preference union men without work.

HUGHIE: So, no work for us non-union men the day again.

JOHN: The work's not there—

HUGHIE: John, I'm gettin' fed up standin' outside that gate every mornin' while youse all get the pick of the work. I've only got four days in three weeks.

JOHN: What can you do when the work's not there?

HUGHIE: Open the books and let me into the union.

JOHN: I think there's a meetin' about that today.

[*They both turn and walk towards the exit.*]

HUGHIE: Well, you've got on to the union committee for the first time, John. We're all expectin' some changes.

JOHN: Who do you think I am—Houdini?

[*They exit.*]

SCENE 2

The scene is at the dockside. JOHN GRAHAM *and* MCKIBBEN *enter pushing a hand-truck. A heave, made up of six bags of grain rests on the truck. A hook is lowered from the ship. The men hook on the heave which then disappears offstage. Leg McNamara's voice is heard offstage.*

LEG: Houl' on down there a minute!

MCKIBBEN: Don't tell me that winch's broke down again!

JOHN: Looks very like it.

LEG: Need any ropes down there?

MCKIBBEN: Never mind the ropes! Get that winch movin' till we get away outta here!

LEG: What do you want me to do? I'm only drivin' the thing, I didn't build it!

JOHN: I thought you knew all about winches!

LEG: Ach, away and laugh at your ma!

[MCKIBBEN *sits down on the truck.*]

MCKIBBEN: We'll never get away the day.

[LEG MCNAMARA *enters. He wears thick, oily gloves.*]

LEG: It'll not be long till it's fixed, lads. Candyapple Docherty's helpin' the ships's engineer to fix the winch. [*He laughs.*]

MCKIBBEN: We'll never get away the day.

JOHN: What time is it, Leg?

LEG: Nearly eleven a'clock. Is there much cargo left?

JOHN: Only another half-a-dozen heaves, no more.

LEG: That's not so bad.

MCKIBBEN: If that winch wouldn't keep breakin' down, we could've been away long go.

LEG: There's the two of yiz shop stewards. Away and do something about it.

JOHN: There's a bit of a difference between bein' a shop steward and a ship's engineer.

LEG: Oh, it's alright. Here's the union chairman. Jack Henry'll get things movin'. What about ye, Jack? [JACK HENRY *enters.*]

HENRY: What's wrong here?

MCKIBBEN: Winch's broke down, Jack.

LEG: For the umpteenth time.

JOHN: But we shouldn't be too long. There's only another half-a-dozen heaves left.

HENRY: If the winch gets fixed! That's what's wrong with too many people at this dock. Easy come, easy go. This is all work and we've had to fight hard and sore to get it over the years. Sometimes I think some of you dockers don't know the half of it.

JOHN: What should we know, then?

HENRY: Well, for a start, there's two unions round here and it hasn't always been easy to keep the lion's share of the work away from themens.

JOHN: You mean the Protestant section?

MCKIBBEN: They're based in England and our union's based in Dublin.

JOHN: But why has no one ever found a solution to the problem of two unions at Belfast docks?

HENRY: There's always been two unions. That's the way things are and always will be.

MCKIBBEN: I think the solution's simple. Always do a deal with the employers beforehand, so that we get any disputed work, even if it means doin' the job at a cheaper rate. At least it ensures we get it.

JOHN: And you regard yourself as a trade unionist?

MCKIBBEN: Why not?

JOHN: Because any trade unionist can see that the present situation, whereby the employers can play the work off two unions, wouldn't arise if we were one, strong union. Catholic dockers and Protestant dockers. That's common sense.

HENRY: Common sense, my arse. Our job goes no further than to protect the rights of our members. Against the Protestant union, if that's necessary.

JOHN: But they're trade unionists, too. Two unions at Belfast docks defeats the very purpose of organised labour. Larkin didn't ask anybody's religion when he led the workers of Belfast to bring the city to a standstill in 1907. How it ever got to the stage of two unions I'll never know.

MCKIBBEN: Because they're Protestants and we're Catholics.

JOHN: But we're all dockers.

MCKIBBEN: That's got nothin' to do with it.

LEG: Maybe somebody should approach the other crowd about all of us coming together.

HENRY: What do you know about anything?

LEG: I was only makin' a suggestion, Jack.

HENRY: That's another thing. Too many people have too much to say round here. We're all followers of our union founders, Larkin and Connolly, but we have to be practical.

[*Enter* BUCKETS MCGUINNESS]

BUCKETS: What's all the yellin' about? Is the new committee fightin' among themselves already? Is the new member causin' trouble? Have you been spakin' up, John Graham?

MCKIBBEN: Shut up, McGuinness. What do you know?

BUCKETS: Shut up, m'bollocks! What? You? I'm round this dock long before you, your da or anybody belonging to you. [MCKIBBEN *attempts to go for* BUCKETS *but* HENRY *waves him back.*] Oh, he wants to bate me for sayin' the wrong things. It would annoy you to think the dockers is askin' questions for a change. Questions like will the committee be able to handle John Graham?

JOHN: Scrub it, Buckets!

BUCKETS: Or as I heard one docker say the other day, 'Can we now expect to see the union return to what it used to be under Jim Larkin and Connolly?'

LEG: But Connolly's union we are and us Belfast dockers'll carry on with the worst wages and conditions in any port, British or Irish.

HENRY: Watch it, Leg. You're luckin' a son into the union.

[LEG *is extremely embarrassed.*]

BUCKETS: That's what I like about our union. They would never be personal about union affairs. Well, I can say whatever the hell I like. I have no sons, nor do I crawl to anybody for work. What? I wouldn't lower myself.

MCKIBBEN: There's neither work nor want in ye.

BUCKETS: For once in your life, McKibben, you're right. If I had the inclination to work I'd have to lick the arse of people like you and I'd rather stand up in Barney's any day firin' liquor into me. If work was any good, the wealthy would be doin' it.

MCKIBBEN: You're only a drunkard.

BUCKETS: A happy drunkard. And I'd rather be a happy drunkard than a sweat-arsed, work-drunk, mealy-mouthed, nothin'-to-show-for-it dock labourer. Leg, I want to see you about a few shillins.

HENRY: That suits you, McGuinness. C'mon, McKibben, to we see what's wrong with this winch. By the way, Graham, there's a union meetin' at dinner-hour, to decide on whether or not to open the union for more members. [*Exit* MCKIBBEN *and* HENRY.]

BUCKETS: There goes our two union leaders. There's more brains in a bucket of skins.

LEG: Did you hear Henry to me? Jasus, you'd think I was askin' for somethin' I'm not entitled to. A man should be able to spake his mind even if he wanted twenty sons into the union.

BUCKETS: I thought you had a son in, Leg.

LEG: The eldest lad, Hughie, he shoulda been in. The union books closed two days before he left school and he's pushin' thirty nigh.

JOHN: Is that how long it is since the union books were open? You wouldn't think it.

LEG: It is strange the way the dock works. You can't get in unless you're in the union and you can't get into the union unless you're da was a docker before ye.

JOHN: I'm sure it seems a bit unfair to the outsider.

LEG: The outsider! What about my sons? My Hughie's workin' non-union round here nigh for years and me 33 years round the place.

BUCKETS. That's because certain union men have no sons and don't want the books open and you know it, Leg.

LEG: I know it only too well and the whole dock's talkin' about it. They've left it that long nigh that men's gonna be fightin' over who gets in and who doesn't. As well as Hughie, Danny-boy's luckin' in. He's only 22, but he insists that he should get the button cause he's gettin' married.

JOHN: The oldest son always gets the button.

LEG: Easier said than done. I don't know what I'm gonna do.

[*Enter* HUGHIE MCNAMARA.]

HUGHIE: Da, da, did you hear there's gonna be a union meetin' the day about openin' the union books?

LEG: I heard alright.

HUGHIE: Well, c'mon with me, da, till I get my name down.

LEG: Take your time, Hughie. Give is a chance to get the thing sorted out.

HUGHIE: What do you mean, take m'time, da? I'm waitin' years for this and you tell me to take m'time?

[*Enter* DANNY-BOY.]

DANNY-BOY: You better not. I want that button.

HUGHIE: I'm the oldest son, it's mine.

DANNY-BOY: I need the money, I'm gettin' married. Right, da?

LEG: Of course, you're gettin' married, Danny-boy, but Hughie is the oldest between the two of ye.

DANNY-BOY: What? Are you makin' differences nigh between your own sons? He's better than me?

LEG: I'm not, I'm not!

DANNY-BOY: That's alright. I'm no good. As long as I know the way of it.

LEG: It's not that way a'tall.

DANNY-BOY: What way is it, then?

JOHN: You've got it all wrong, Danny. Your da's only doin' his best. As you know, it is the usual system round here that the oldest always has first option.

DANNY-BOY: Oh, yiz are all against me nigh!

LEG: No, we're not, we're just—

DANNY-BOY: Just nothin'! Da, I want a decision from you. Nigh! I'm savin' up to get married. I need to know.

HUGHIE: You're not on.

DANNY-BOY: Neither are you.

JOHN: Look, why don't the two of yiz leave it for a while, sit down later and discuss the whole thing quietly with your da?

LEG: That's what I've been tryin' to tell them.

HUGHIE: There's no discussin' about it. *I'm* the oldest.

DANNY-BOY: Who do you think you are?

BUCKETS: Hold on a minute, lads. There's a very simple way round this.

LEG: What are you talkin' about?

BUCKETS: Toss up.

JOHN: You couldn't do that.

HUGHIE [*sarcastically*]**:** Toss a bloody coin.

LEG: No, that's no way to sort it out.

BUCKETS: Well, if anybody can come up with a better idea, let's hear it? [*Silence*] Right then, let's toss. Heads or tails, Danny-boy?

LEG: I don't like the idea of this.

BUCKETS: It's not your idea, it's mine. Luck, this way both sons have an equal chance. Have yiz no sense? What? Otherwise, there'll be blood and snatters. Call, Danny-boy?

DANNY-BOY: Heads.

BUCKETS: Right! All's it needs is a bit of commonsense. Up it goes. [*He tosses the coin up in the air. The others stand intently as he lifts it off the floor.*] I'm afraid it's tails, Danny-boy. And the new holder of a button in the Dockers union is ... Hughie McNamara.

DANNY-BOY: I'm not wearin' that, da. No toss of a coin's keepin' me outiv work.

HUGHIE: You were bate fair and square.

DANNY-BOY: M'da's gonna decide who gets it, not that. N'that, right, da?

HUGHIE: Crawlin' to your daddy nigh? Ya wee boy ye.

DANNY-BOY: I'm no wee boy.

HUGHIE: You're a big chile.

LEG: C'mon, Hughie, that's enough.

HUGHIE: He's a big baby.

LEG: I said knock it on the head.

DANNY-BOY: I'm warnin' you, Hughie

HUGHIE: Aye, you'd break a lot of delph.

DANNY-BOY: Da!

[DANNY-BOY *lunges, fists poised.* HUGHIE *responds likewise.*]

HUGHIE: C'mon, try it ... son!

LEG: Hughie!

JOHN: Scrub it, lads.

HUGHIE: He's only a wee boy.

DANNY-BOY: Am A?

[DANNY-BOY *throws a punch.*]

LEG: Jesus Christ, stop it!

[*The two brothers wrestle and end up rolling on the floor, while* LEG *and* JOHN *attempt to separate them.* BUCKETS *discreetly exits as* JOHN *eventually manages to pull* HUGHIE *off* DANNY-BOY.]

HUGHIE: Don't you think this is over. I'll make you sorry for that!

[HUGHIE *walks off.*]

DANNY-BOY: Any time!

LEG: Shut up, for Jasis sake, will ya?

JOHN: That's out of order, Danny. You wanna catch yourself on.

[MCKIBBEN *enters.*]

MCKIBBEN: What's goin' on here?

LEG: Nothin'. Right, you! [*To* DANNY-BOY] Aren't you workin' in the next hatch?

DANNY-BOY: Aye.

LEG: Well, get back to it. If Jimmy Sweeney sees you standin' about here, you'll be sacked.

DANNY-BOY: I'm goin'.

LEG: And let that be the end of it. Imagine two brothers fightin' each other? [DANNY-BOY *exits.*]

MCKIBBEN: What is goin' on here?

JOHN: Leg's sons were fightin' over who's gettin' into the union.

MCKIBBEN: I've said it all along. The books should never be opened.

LEG: I can't do anything about it, Harry. Both of them needs work.

MCKIBBEN: The might get a quare shock if none of them gets in.

[*Enter* JIMMY SWEENEY.]

SWEENEY: C'mon a that, w'yiz! We haven't all day to get this cargo shifted. I've anor hatch on this boat to luck after. [LEG *exits.* JOHN *lifts the shafts of the truck and begins to move off, followed by* MCKIBBEN. LEG *hurries off towards the ship.*] C'mon, yiz are workin' for yourselves here!

SCENE 3

BARNEY MCGIVERN *is on duty behind the bar of his public house. Dominated by an old-fashioned wooden counter, the pub is anything but luxurious. At one end of the bar is a small enclosed snug, while a six-foot high partition at the other end hides a single standing place at the bar.* BUCKETS MCGUINNESS *is standing at the bar with the proverbial glass of wine at his fingertips.* THERESA GRAHAM *enters.*

THERESA: Sorry I'm late, Barney, but I didn't know the time goin' in this mornin'. Hiya, Buckets.

BUCKETS: What about ye, Theresa daughter?

BARNEY: Never worry, girl, never worry.

THERESA: That's what's wrong with me, I worry too much. There was me runnin' the feet off myself to get John Graham's dinner ready and him never showed up for it. I'll go for the pies nigh, Barney, and clean the place up when I come back. Will that be alright?

BARNEY: Please yourself. I'm not particular one way or the other.

THERESA: I wonder where John is to this time?

BUCKETS: Probably still at the first meetin' of the new shop stewards committee. You're married to a top man in the union nigh.

THERESA: Oh, don't I know? That's all I've heard from him since he was elected last week. It's all you get from you get up in the mornin' till you go to bed at night. Union, union, union! Will I get the usual two dozen, Barney?

BARNEY: Should be enough, Theresa.

THERESA: Right, I'll see yiz later then.

BUCKETS: Cheerio.

[THERESA *exits.* BUCKETS *drains his glass and looks at* BARNEY.]

BUCKETS: Barney a ... I'm not very strong at the minute, do you a ... do you think you could work me a drink on strap?

BARNEY: Not on your life. At least not until you pay me the bill you've already run up.

BUCKETS: But sure, there's a rubber boat due in ...

[SARAH MONTAGUE *enters from the snug and walks to the bar.*]

SARAH: Is there no sign of your woman yet, Barney?

BARNEY: Not yet.

SARAH: I don't know why she goes near that pawn. He gives her no more than buttons.

BUCKETS: Ah nigh, go on Sarah Montague. If you were handed one odd boot and a clock with no hands on it, you wouldn't pay out either.

SARAH: Who's talkin' to you? Didn't your missis try an' pawn a paintin' of Robert Emmett?

BUCKETS: What was wrong with that?

SARAH: Nothin'. Except she painted it herself. Give is a wee gin, Barney. [MARY-ANN MCKEOWN *enters.*] Where the hell were you?

MARY-ANN: Oh Sarah dear, you don't know the trouble I've had this day. When I got up this mornin', that lazy blurt wouldn't go out to his work without his five Woodbine. Then our Rosie came round luckin' the loan of a pound. God, Sarah, I hadn't got it to give to her. Not this week anyway.

SARAH: But did you go up to the other place? Give is a wee sherry as well, Barney.

MARY-ANN: Don't mention it. Tryin' to get money up there's like tryin' to tell a Protestant King Billy's horse wasn't white.

SARAH: Well, that's not as bad as tryin' to tell a Papist that Patrick Pearse used bad language nigh an' again.

BUCKETS: Would you listen to the two of them. I don't know how youse two sit in that box without tearin' the hair out of one anor.

SARAH [*lifting her drink*]: As long as you and your likes aren't there, Buckets McGuinness, we'll do alright. C'mon, Mary-Ann, I think we should discuss our financial matters in private.

MARY-ANN: Whatever you like nigh, Sarah, it's all the same to me.

SARAH: You'd think the proprietor of this establishment would be more careful who he let into this public house. Dacent customers could be offended. [*Exit* SARAH *to snug.*]

MARY-ANN: Don't take any heed of her, Buckets son, she's only a oul' nark.

BUCKETS: Don't worry, I don't. [MARY-ANN *exits to snug.*] Well, there you are nigh, Barney. Them two's away to discuss their financial matters in private. Ha, the laugh of it. Half bloody Sailortown knows their financial matters and more. I heard two shipyard men from Ballymacarrett at the dogs last night talkin' about the money the owe Sarah Montague.

BARNEY: Ah, she's not the worst. There's moneylenders in this town, as you well know, who'd watch you dyin' in the street afore they'd lend you something, if you weren't clear with them.

BUCKETS: Aye, and them the best chapelgoers in the city. Well, I'm gonna put that to the test, Barney. I owe Sarah Montague 18 shillins this long time and I'm gonna put the hammer on her nigh. [BUCKETS *goes over to the snug.*] Sarah! Sarah Montague, could I spake to you for a minute?

SARAH [*shouting from the box*]: Go away. You still owe me 18 shillins!

BUCKETS: But Mrs. Montague, I was wantin' to talk to you about that very thing! [SARAH *enters, very stern looking as usual*] Mrs. Montague, I a ... well, I had nothin' to lift this week and the wife's luckin' a few hapens ... but there's a timber boat due in tomorrow and I'm a cert to be over the hatch for Big O'Connor, so I'll have at least two days pay to lift next week.

SARAH: You're a confounded liar!

[*She turns to exit but* BUCKETS *grabs her by the shoulder.*]

BUCKETS: Mrs. Montague, I swear on our Paddy's life, I'll pay you back next week.

SARAH: Sure, your Paddy's one fut on the grave as it is ...

BUCKETS: Luck, Mrs. Montague, I'm tellin' you the God's honest truth, Big O'Connor always gives me a job over the hatch at a—

SARAH: You can Big O'Connor me till you're blue in the face. The answer is NO! [*She exits and slams the door behind her.* BUCKETS *slowly returns to the bar.*]

BARNEY: Bad luck, Buckets.

BUCKETS: And you said she wasn't the worst. Barney a ... Listen, give is one wine and I'll fix you up on Thursday?

BARNEY: Man dear, you're the limit. I can't!

[*Enter* SARAH.]

SARAH: Here's a pound, you, and if that isn't paid by Thursday, along with the 18 shillins, you've had it!

BUCKETS: Ach, thanks very much, Mrs. Montague. Sure you know you'll get every penny of it as soon as the wages office opens on the the dot. Thanks.

SARAH: Thursday!

[SARAH *exits. Buckets' face lights up. He kisses the pound note.*]

BUCKETS: Make that a double wine, Barney. And a ... bring her over her usual.

BARNEY: I told you she's not the worst.

BUCKETS: Naa. But she's still an oul'"—[LEG MCNAMARA *enters*] Ach, bully Leg, what about ye? What are ye havin'?

LEG: Bottle a stout. Where'd you get the money? It must be ... the day the two of us got into the union together, since you last bought me a drink. Mind thon day up in Hannigan's Bar? You vomited all over North Queen Street.

BUCKETS: Give over, Leg. Take a bottle of stout an' shut up. Will you take a halfin?

LEG: No, this'll do me. M'head's bustin'. I was on the whiskey all last night round in Peter's. I don't suppose any of the Dock Committee's been in yet?

BARNEY: Not yet. What is it—problems?

LEG: Did he not tell ye? The two sons was fightin' down at the boat this mornin' over which one of thems gettin' into the union.

BARNEY: I don't believe you!

BUCKETS: Ach, what are you worried about, isn't it all settled nigh? Didn't I handle the whole thing like a master?

LEG: It was you that started them fightin'. Barney, he tossed up a coin an' all hell broke loose.

BARNEY: Sure, Leg, you shoulda known better than to let Buckets McGuinness near anything.

BUCKETS: Is that the thanks you get for tryin' to be helpful. It is sorted out, isn't it?

LEG: Some chance.

BARNEY: You've problems there, Leg.

BUCKETS: Not as bad as mine. I've to get Sarah Montague 38 shillins by Thursday.

BARNEY: Did I not hear you tellin' her you were goin' to be workin' at a timber boat?

BUCKETS: For Jasis sake, Barney! How long do you know me now? There's a timber boat due in alright but if you catch me near it give me a good boot up the arse and chase me home. No, no, don't chase me home. That's where the wife is. I owe her money as well. [BUCKETS *slaps* LEG *on the shoulder and has a good laugh at the idea.*] You're never safe no matter where you go. I often wonder where we'd all be the day if our oul' lads hadna been dockers. If I could a just changed the K for a T things mighta been different as a doctor's son.

LEG: You've no guarantee.

BUCKETS: Maybe you're right. Maybe we're not so badly off the way we are.

LEG: We've John Graham on the committee nigh, maybe we're on the threshold of a new era. A new period of change.

BARNEY: Nobody'll ever change the dock—it's too set in its ways.

LEG: Oh, I don't know. Young Graham's a lad of some ability and he's a very determined kid. Hasn't he spent the last five years to get where he is nigh against stiff opposition?

BUCKETS: Is right. But there's a certain element who have the habit of turnin' the most conscientious union man into an employers' lickspittle overnight. Luck, I'll tell you what I'll do. Where's that oul' photo of the first Union Executive with Larkin and Connolly in it?

BARNEY: I think it's down there somewhere.

BUCKETS: Give is it up here. [BARNEY *bends down below the bar and comes up with an old framed photograph which he hands to* BUCKETS.] Nigh that somebody with a bit of wit is shop steward in the Irish Transport & General Workers' Union, Docks Section, we might see a return to the union these men helped to build. [BUCKETS *walks to the end of the bar where he takes down a calendar and replaces it with the photograph.*] Up ya go and I hope to Jasis we can keep ye up there with the help of John Graham.

LEG: As long as he doesn't bow the knee to no employer or no union henchmen, he'll have our full backing. Mines anyway.

BUCKETS: Well, time'll tell the story. Here, Leg! [BUCKETS *holds up his empty glass.*] It's your turn to buy this downtrodden, underpaid dock labourer a drink. [*Speaking politely*] I'll have a wine please, thank you.

LEG: A wine, Barney, and a bottle of stout for myself. Hey, I wonder will John call in afore he goes home. I'm bustin' to know if the books is gettin' opened.

BARNEY: I'd imagine he'd be in shortly. The meetin'll hardly last all day.

BUCKETS: They're probably cuttin' the water outiv him. I didn't wanna say it in front of his wee girl, but he'll have a rough time with the Jack Henrys of this world.

LEG: Well, there's an awful lot of men's pinnin' their hopes on him.

BUCKETS: I hate to say it, but the might as well pin their hopes on the Vatican givin' some of their priceless paintins to the starvin' people of India. I hope I'm wrong.

[JOHN GRAHAM *enters.*]

LEG: There's the man himself.

BUCKETS: What about ye, son?

JOHN: Dead on, lads. Give us a bottle of stout, Barney.

BARNEY: Alright, John.

LEG: Well, how did the first meetin' go? Did yiz decide on openin' the books?

JOHN: Just about. I don't think there'll be too many gettin' in, though.

LEG: Is that right?

JOHN: Is it Hughie you're puttin' in, then?

LEG: I don't know what to do.

JOHN: Still fightin', are they?

LEG: Wouldn't you know.

JOHN: That's bad. Is there no way of sortin' it out—since Buckets' magic formula didn't exactly have them shakin' hands?

LEG: I'll have to think of something.

JOHN: Do you think it might help if I had a word with Hughie?

LEG: Would ye, John?

JOHN: I'm not sayin' I'll solve the problem, but I'll have a yarn with him anyway.

BUCKETS: And I could have a talk with Danny-boy. [LEG *glares at* BUCKETS.] For Jasis sake, Leg, to luck at you, you'd think I was the devil himself.

LEG: Just stay outiv it!

BUCKETS: I know Danny-boy well—

LEG: Haven't you done enough damage? Just stay outiv it!

[SARAH *and* MARY-ANN *enter from the snug.*]

SARAH: What nigh is all the shoutin' about?

BUCKETS: Nothin' much. Leg and me give two Brethern from York Road Orange Lodge a bit of a kickin' last night and we were just debatin' who done the most damage.

SARAH: Huh! You wouldn't have the guts to luck sideways at an Orangeman, never mind lift your hand to two of them. Do you want anor sherry, Mrs. McKeown?

MARY-ANN: Whatever you like nigh. It's all the same to me, Sarah.

SARAH: But it's you that's gonna be ... Ach, it doesn't matter. Give is a gin and a sherry, Barney.

BARNEY: A gin and a sherry comin' up.

MARY-ANN: Do you know what I was thinkin', Sarah?

SARAH: How am I supposed to know what you're thinkin', unless you tell me? [BARNEY *sets up the drink.*]

MARY-ANN: I was thinkin' maybe I should take a wee hot whiskey instead.

SARAH: But sure I ... Oh, it wouldn't be you. You may change that, Barney.

BARNEY: No problem. I'll bring it over to you.

[SARAH *exits to snug, followed by* MARY-ANN *making faces behind her back.*]

BUCKETS: You know, givin' drink to them two's a waste of time.

LEG: How?

BUCKETS: They never get drunk.

BARNEY: As long as the keep spendin'.

JOHN: They've too much talkin' to catch up on ...

[THERESA GRAHAM *enters excitedly.*]

THERESA: Is John Graham here ... Oh God, John, there's been an accident at the dock!

JOHN: What happened?

LEG: Was there anybody hurt?

THERESA: Mr. McNamara, it was your young fella.

LEG: Danny-boy!

THERESA: Yes, Danny-boy.

LEG: Jesis, Mary and Joseph!

THERESA: But I don't think he's badly hurt. Just something with his arm.

LEG: Where is he nigh?

THERESA: Oh, he's away to the hospital an' all.

LEG: Are you sure it was just his arm?

THERESA: I was talkin' to Scrub A'Nail in Pilot Street. He said he was

workin' along with him and he seemed to think he wasn't too
bad a'tall.

LEG: I may go up to the hospital anyway. Which one is it, do you know?

THERESA: The Mater.

JOHN: Aye, you might be as well goin' on up, Leg, and seein' him
anyway.

BUCKETS: Do you want me to go along with ye?

LEG: I'll be alright. [LEG *exits.*]

JOHN: How did this happen, Theresa, did you hear?

THERESA: Aye, Scrub said it was an overloaded heave fell on him in
the houl' of the boat.

JOHN: Oh, overloadin' heaves? That's Jimmy Sweeney again. He was
bossin' that boat.

BUCKETS: There's bosses round here and they'd put three times the
begs into heaves if they could get away with it.

JOHN: Aye, and dockers who'd do it without a word of protest.

BUCKETS: All to get away that wee bit earlier.

BARNEY: It couldn't be safe standin' under a bundle of begs when it's
swingin' up in the air above ye. Especially if they're overloaded.

THERESA: God, I near died when I heard there was somebody hurt
at the dock. My heart was in my mouth thinkin' it was this fella.
Know the way you always think the worst.

BARNEY: It's been a right fright for you. It seems to me there's far too
many accidents at that dock. It's a wonder there isn't more killed.

THERESA: Like everything else. They'll wait till some poor
unfortunate bein' gets killed and then they'll do something.

BUCKETS: It wouldn't be the first. I mind the day we stood and
watched a man sinkin' slowly in the houl' of a grain boat.

JOHN: Why didn't yiz get in and get him out?

BUCKETS: There was any amount of us in the houl', shovellin' hell
for lyre. But the more we shovelled, the more he sank. And we
couldn't pull him out, his head woulda left his shoulders.

THERESA: Oh my God!

BUCKETS: We even had time to get a priest down to give the poor man
the last rites. A slow, slow death. That was the first and last time I
ever saw a crowd of dockers standin' weepin' into their caps.

JOHN: It's hard to believe, Buckets, yiz couldn't get him out.

BUCKETS: I know, but it's true. You ask any of the oul' dockers.

THERESA: Don't be goin' on, yiz'll have me more worried than I am
already. I don't know how yiz stick it!

JOHN: We're not gonna stick it any longer. I've already had it out with the union about safety regulations at the dock and I'm gonna insist on some action against Jimmy Sweeney.

BUCKETS: There's planty of dockers has a thing or two to say about him. Sure, there's not a man about the place would have a drink with him. He sits his life alone in the canteen takin' his tea and then slinks about the job spyin' on the men. Would you do it, eh? Not a bit of wonder the talk about him.

JOHN: About him, Buckets, but not to his face and that's what's wrong. His name'll be top of the agenda tomorrow mornin'. That's the first thing I wanna see stopped. Overloadin' heaves. We don't want any more accidents.

[JIMMY SWEENEY *enters. Amidst silence, he walks straight over to the single place behind the partition at the end of the bar. He orders a drink. All eyes turn on* JOHN GRAHAM. *He takes a deep breath and steps out into the middle of the bar.* THERESA *attempts to restrain him.*]

THERESA: Not nigh, John.

JOHN: It's alright, Theresa, it's alright. Sweeney! Jimmy Sweeney, I wanna have a word with you!

[SWEENEY *takes his time appearing.*]

SWEENEY: Whadaya want, Graham?

JOHN: I'm lettin' you know, I'm raisin' your name with the committee first thing in the mornin'. You've been responsible for an injury to a young docker.

SWEENEY: Sure, he was only a non-union man.

JOHN: That's immaterial. I'm raisin' your name.

SWEENEY: Do whatever the fuck you like!

JOHN: I'm warnin' you, you'll not get away with it.

SWEENEY: Luck, I didn't sling the heave, so don't come slabberin' to me, Graham. Blame the dockers who made up the heave.

JOHN: You were the boss. You told them, three extra begs in each heave.

SWEENEY: Crap! Nigh, will you go away and give my head peace?

JOHN: That's exactly what I won't do. There'll be no peace for you while I'm on the committee.

SWEENEY: I'm tremblin'. [SWEENEY *exits behind the partition.* JOHN, *seething with anger, turns and pauses before exiting hurriedly.*]

JOHN: C'mon, Theresa, before I lose my temper!

[*As* JOHN *and* THERESA *are about to exit,* LEG *enters with* MCKIBBEN.]

LEG: Oh, John, Danny-boy's alright. Harry here tells me he only sprained his arm.

JOHN: That's good. Maybe Harry'll do something about *him*!

[JOHN *and* THERESA *exit.*]

MCKIBBEN: What's wrong with him?

BUCKETS: He's only after having a row with Jimmy Sweeney about the accident.

MCKIBBEN: Aye, Graham'd know all about accidents. I better have a word with Jimmy. [MCKIBBEN *exits behind the partition.*]

BARNEY: I'm glad to hear the lad's alright, Leg.

LEG: Aye, it's nothin' to worry about. He'll be out of the hospital afore six a'clock. One of the begs fell on his arm.

BUCKETS: Coulda been his head.

LEG: I know. McKibben's havin' a word with him about it nigh. I can't have that bastard Sweeney. [*McKibben's voice is heard.*]

MCKIBBEN: Barney! Give Jimmy a bottle and a halfin.

BARNEY: Right you be.

BUCKETS: Havin' a word with him's right. He's fixin' himself up for a job in the mornin'. That's a union man for ye.

LEG: Ach, I suppose I should've known.

BUCKETS: You've always known, Leg. The only man who'll try and stand up for the dockers nigh is John Graham. He didn't half give it to Sweeney here a while ago.

LEG: John shoulda hit the glipe. I wish I was young again, there'd be two John Grahams.

BUCKETS: Aye, you'd shite coalbrick if you'd a square arsehole!

[SWEENEY *and* MCKIBBEN *enter, moving towards the exit.*]

MCKIBBEN: It's the dockers' own faults. Half of them doesn't even know how to sling a heave.

SWEENEY: You can say that again. Hey, McNamara!

LEG: What's that, Jimmy?

SWEENEY: I'm startin' a gang for the Dutch boat in the mornin'. I need a man for over-the-hatch.

LEG: Well, I'll be out in the mornin', Jimmy. Is there much cargo?

SWEENEY: Enough to get us four days outiv it.

LEG: That's dead on, Jimmy, I'll be out. See you in the mornin'. [*As* SWEENEY *and* MCKIBBEN *are about to exit,* LEG *calls* SWEENEY *to the side.*] Oh Jimmy! Forget about that accident. I know it was nothin' to do with you. The young lad's right as rain anyway.

SWEENEY: Well, you better tell that other Comanche Graham that. And when you're at it, tell him I said very few foremen like to employ agitators.

MCKIBBEN: And I'll be raisin' *his* name at the next meetin'.

SWEENEY: It's changed times round here, when wee lads is gonna bate ye.

[*They exit.*]

BUCKETS: Up the workers, Leg, eh?

LEG: Whadaya on about?

BUCKETS: Two John Grahams?

LEG: Buckets, you must take the work when it's goin'.

BUCKETS: So, while John Graham's goin' round fightin' for the likes a you, you're cuttin' the feet from below him?

LEG: Luck, it wasn't me invented the system round here. That's the way it's always been.

BUCKETS: It is corruption.

LEG: That's life. I'm fed up tellin' our Hughie. Trade unions, militancy, fightin' talk and all the rest of it's only for buck-ejits. At the end of the day, it's all about puttin' bread on the table. The childer can't eat speeches.

BUCKETS: Scrub the union then?

LEG: It's alright John Graham talkin' about the union, but the union doesn't pay my wages. You have to luck after number one. Nobody's gonna come throwin' loaves a bread at ye. Anyway, I may get up to the house and let the missus know about Danny-boy. That'll be another blurtin' and cryin' match.

BUCKETS: You're lucky it wasn't his head.

LEG: I know. See ya later. [LEG *exits.*]

BUCKETS: Barney, did you ever hear of the Kamikazzi pilots durin' the war? Watch this. [*He walks towards the snug.*]

BARNEY: Where are you goin'?

BUCKETS: I owe the wife three pounds and I have to go home sometime. Here goes. Sarah! Mrs. Montague, could I have a wee word with you?

SARAH: Have you got my 38 shillins?

BUCKETS: Yes! [*He winces as the publican looks astounded.* SARAH *enters.*]

SARAH: Where is it?

BUCKETS: Well, I don't exactly have it on me at the moment ... but [SARAH *turns to go, but he grabs hold of her arm.*] ... what I mean, Mrs. Montague, is ... I have a brand new suit in the pawn. The wife only bought me it at Easter. The best a sweg it is. Nigh, if you could lend me three pounds sterling to lift it, I could then sell it to you. You could then take the three pound and the 38 shillins outiv it and since the suit's worth a good tenner, you'd only owe me five pounds two shillins. Nigh, don't worry. I'd give you plenty of time to pay me.

SARAH: How the hell did you work that one out?

BUCKETS: The suit, Mrs. Montague, the suit. It's a foreign make, worth twenty pound to you.

SARAH: What do you mean, foreign?

BUCKETS: Made in Douglas, Isle of Man. Nothin' but the best.

SARAH: I'm sure. There's no way I'd give you this money if I didn't think there was a suit there. But here, take that three pound and get me that suit back here straight away.

BUCKETS: Fifteen minutes, Mrs. Montague, I'll not be any more than 15 minutes. [SARAH *exits.*]

BARNEY: I don't know anybody that can get money off her like you. But here, you may rush up and lift that suit afore the pawn closes. [BUCKETS *takes a long drink.*]

BUCKETS: What suit? [*He exits.*]

SCENE 4

The scene is the Graham home. A small, terraced kitchen-house. No illusions of grandeur, but neat. JOHN GRAHAM *enters carrying a tray containing a teapot, cups, sugar etc. He switches on the television and sits down.*

HUGHIE: John! Are you there, John?
    [HUGHIE MCNAMARA *knocks on the door and enters.*]

JOHN: Come on in, Hughie.

HUGHIE: Did you hear about the accident to our Danny-boy? He's in hospital.

JOHN: I did, aye. Wanna cup of tea? [*He hands* HUGHIE *a cup of tea.*]

HUGHIE: Thanks, John. An overloaded heave fell on his arm.

JOHN: Jimmy Sweeney, you mean.

HUGHIE: That's a bastard. We'll have to do something about him, John. Our D-B could be lyin' dead the day.

JOHN: How is he anyway?

HUGHIE: I phoned up. He's alright. Gettin' out shortly, the said. Have you a wee drop of sugar, John?

JOHN: Sorry, Hughie. Here.

HUGHIE: John, what are we gonna do about foremen like Sweeney? And our union leaders aren't much better, McKibben and Jack Henry.

JOHN: Did you know that Sweeney was once on the committee?

HUGHIE: I didn't know—but from what I hear that seems to be the way too many of the committee have went over the years.

JOHN: Simple. Most of the guys who go on the committee have no politics.

HUGHIE: You reckon politics is essential to be a shop steward?

JOHN: You need politics to go into frontline conflict with the employers. If you don't know the wider picture, them boys can charm you inside out.

HUGHIE: I'd like to see them tryin' it with me.

JOHN: Could you resist the offer of a well-paid, regular job? 'Cause that's the first tactic the use to get rid of the best shop stewards.

HUGHIE: How would you handle that type of bribe?

JOHN: Well, for a start, it wouldn't come as a surprise to me. I know what I'm doin' at the bargainin' table. I know I'm representin' workers. And I know what the men on the other side of the table represent. Themselves, profit, money in the bank. Hughie, unless you're conscious of that goin' in, you're a batin docket.

HUGHIE: That sounds great, John, but not everybody understands that.

JOHN: Not a bit a wonder. Because we're all brain-washed with the platitudes and phrases the employers come off with in their newspapers. [JOHN *mimics an upper-class voice.*] 'We want to provide jobs for the community ... our main concern is to provide a service.' It would make you sick to listen to it when you know that an employer sets up to do one thing—make money— nothin' more and nothin' less.

HUGHIE: But some of the committee do their best.

JOHN: A lot of nice, well-meanin' guys become shop stewards. But it's like getting into the ring with Sonny Liston. They've no chance of winnin'.

HUGHIE: Well, as you say, our union leadership doesn't seem to have any great politics.

JOHN: Not only do they not have any Labour politics, but they'll resist anything radical at every turn. Larkin and Connolly, how are ye!

HUGHIE: I don't suppose McKibben and Henry are too happy about you?

JOHN: There's been nothin' said to me. But McKibben has told a couple of dockers that if Graham comes off with any 'red talk', as he puts it, I'd be for the chop.

HUGHIE: McKibben's bad news.

JOHN: He's only the message-boy. Jack Henry pulls the strings.

HUGHIE: Do you think there's ever any chance of Henry ever improvin'?

JOHN: I don't know. He's not an expert on exactly what dynamics influence the world of high finance, but he's not stupid either.

HUGHIE: He must know changes are long overdue at the dock.

JOHN: Yes, but the question is, will it suit him to bring them in?

HUGHIE: Time will tell. Which reminds me what I called round for. It's time you lent me that book you promised. *The Ragged Trousered* something ...

JOHN: Oh yes, I forgot about that. It should be over here somewhere, I think. [JOHN *begins to search a small bookshelf while* HUGHIE *stands watching the television*] Are you readin' anything at the moment?

HUGHIE: You'll never guess.

JOHN: I give up.

HUGHIE: *Lady Chatterley's Lover.*

JOHN: Very nice, but hardly what you'd call enlightenin' stuff.

HUGHIE: But in a way it is, John. I lap up the idea of a gamekeeper touchin' for the Lady of the Manor. Just like my ambiton to have a skelp at Princess Margaret. Know what I mean? Pauper meets princess and all that stuff. It definitely sharpens the mind about the class thing.

JOHN: Bringin' sex into politics as usual. No, I can't see that bloody book, Hughie. I'll have a better luck for it later on.

HUGHIE: Well, you can throw it round to me.

JOHN: Tell me this, have you given any more thought to the button thing?

HUGHIE: It's all sorted out.

JOHN: And?

HUGHIE: It's D-B's. That is, if he's not sickened by the accident.

JOHN: Really?

HUGHIE: Well, when it boils down to it, he does need it more than me.

JOHN: That's a good decision. Your da'll be pleased.

HUGHIE: He doesn't know yet. That's where I'm goin' nigh. [THERESA GRAHAM *enters*] Ach, the very woman I'm wantin' to see.

THERESA: There must be something wrong when you wanna see me.

HUGHIE: Oh, there's nothin' wrong. It's just that I'm a ... I'm in the finals of the jivin' competition in the Plaza this Saturday and I was wonderin', I mean, if it's alright with you, John, I was thinkin' maybe, you'd partner me.

THERESA: Me! God save is! What happened Sheila McKenna, did she get fed up you trampin' all over her toes?

HUGHIE: I never tramped on a partner's toes in my life. But I fell out with her after the semi-finals.

THERESA: What happened?

HUGHIE: She wanted me to go to chapel with her.

THERESA: Ahh, that's nice.

HUGHIE: Don't have me usin' bad language! Once a wee girl round this way thinks she's goin' steady with you, the first thing she asks, is for ye to go to chapel with her. If you fall for that, it's confession the followin' week. Here's me to myself, 'Hughie, son, give this woman a by-ball!' What do you say, John, eh?

JOHN: Nothin'.

HUGHIE: You must agree.

JOHN: I'm sayin' nothin', Hughie.

THERESA: He knows better. John always says that when the Catholic Church has the mothers of the country, they've got everybody else.

JOHN: Hughie, you're a witness. I never said a word.

HUGHIE: Right, end of argument. Back to the point. Are you gonna partner me on Saturday night, or what?

THERESA: Don't be silly. It's years since I was even at a dance.

HUGHIE: Aye, but you were good. Sure you won the competition two years in a row. Eh, John?

JOHN: It's up to her.

THERESA: No, Hughie, I don't think so. My dancin' days is over. The only dancin' I do nigh is dance attention to a husband and two kids. But it was nice of you to ask, Hughie. I still say Sheila McKenna is your best bet.

HUGHIE: I told you I'm fed up with her and, anyway—[*Whips out his comb and proceeds to comb his hair*]—if you really wanna know the truth, I got shot of her because she kept wreckin' m'hair.

THERESA: Go on, ya fool ye.

HUGHIE: But who am I gonna get?

JOHN: Have you tried Sarah Montague?

HUGHIE: It's not a wake I'm goin' to. I suppose there's nothin' else for it. I may go and make that phone call.

JOHN: What phone call?

HUGHIE: Connie Francis.

THERESA: What are you on about?

HUGHIE: Who? Me and Connie Francis has a wee thing goin' together. She asked me over to California the last time I was talkin' to her.

JOHN: And why didn't you go?

HUGHIE: I told her I was too busy. I was workin' the weekend at the South African boat. I'm away.

THERESA: You couldn't believe a word comes out of your mouth.

JOHN: Listen, Hughie, I'll have a good luck for that book and send it round to you.

HUGHIE: Okay, see yiz.

THERESA: Cheerio, Hughie. [HUGHIE *exits.*] That's a goodin, eh! Dance with him in a jivin' competition!

JOHN: Sure, you know Hughie McNamara. [JOHN *returns to the bookshelf. He is on his hands and knees.*]

THERESA: What's wrong, have you taken to a fit of prayin'?

JOHN: What? No, I'm luckin' for a book I was gonna lend Hughie.

THERESA: More bloody politics.

JOHN: So what?

THERESA: Do you never get enough? Did Mary come round with the kids?

JOHN: Do you see them?

THERESA: I'm only askin'.

JOHN: Frig it! Did you see that book?

THERESA: What book?

JOHN: *The Ragged Trousered Philanthropists.* It's a thick book with a red cover. By Robert Tressell.

THERESA: The ragged what?

JOHN: Ach, it doesn't matter.

THERESA: You don't have to eat the nose of me.

JOHN: I'm luckin' for a book I left down right there, only yesterday, and nigh it's missin'.

THERESA: Luck, John Graham, if you're in bad form over what's goin' on at the dock, don't take it out on me.

JOHN: What? Who mentioned the dock?

THERESA: Don't try and kid me. You laugh and joke with Hughie McNamara, but I know when there's more on your mind than a book.

JOHN: Okay, so what?

THERESA: So what? It's time we had a talk about this whole thing.

JOHN: Some other time.

THERESA: No, John, nigh.

JOHN: Haven't you still to go round to get the kids outta Mary's?

THERESA: That can wait.

JOHN: Alright. So what are you sayin'?

THERESA: Pack it in.

JOHN: What?

THERESA: I want you off that committee.

JOHN: I'm only on to it.

THERESA: And luck at the trouble it's caused already.

JOHN: But that's what committees are for. So that people can talk and avoid trouble.

THERESA: I want you off it, John.

JOHN: I can't, Theresa. There's things I need to do.

THERESA: Like what?

JOHN: Plenty.

THERESA: Alright, tell me. Tell me what it is that's so important that you absolutely need to do.

JOHN: Luck, Theresa. I work at the dock. Nigh, all's I want to do is work in reasonably acceptable conditions and for a decent wage that will be enough to feed me and you and the kids. Nothin' more and nothin' less.

THERESA: And what about the rest of them? If they aren't shoutin', why do you have to?

JOHN: The rest will shout. Given time.

THERESA: So, in the meantime, you're gonna do enough shoutin' for everybody? While they're all sittin' in pubs laughin' behind your back?

JOHN: I don't care who's laughin' at me. Somebody has to step out from the crowd.

THERESA: Oh aye! Oh aye, you're the big fella in the big picture. John Graham's gonna change in a fortnight what's been goin' on since before he was born?

JOHN: Theresa, you're bein' unreasonable. I just wanna play my part. Honestly and to the best of my ability.

THERESA: What about the rest of them?

JOHN: If I can make the dockers think a bit more about their own situation, as time goes on I think I can get a bit more support.

THERESA: That all sounds very nice, but what about the likes of Harry McKibben? God forgive me for sayin' it but he's no good. If my father was alive the day, he'd have a heart attack to think you were sittin' on the same committee as him.

JOHN: I can't let that come into it.

THERESA: Why? Does my family not mean anything to you?

JOHN: It's union business, Theresa.

THERESA: And what do you call what he done to our Vera?

JOHN: I understand that, but it was a long time ago.

THERESA: Don't you ever think for one minute that we'll forget it.

JOHN: Theresa. The fact that Harry McKibben was seein' your Vera while she was still at school and then left her in trouble can have no bearin' on the present situation.

THERESA: But he was ten years older than her. Ah no! It doesn't matter anymore. We should all forget that Vera isn't here anymore. Her young life lost havin' that bastard's baby and nigh you're sittin' on the same committee as him!

JOHN: I have to, for Jasis sake, I have to!

THERESA: You don't have to!

JOHN: What do I do, then? Walk away? Walk away over something that happened nearly twenty years ago? Something that doesn't directly concern me?

THERESA: Doesn't concern you?

JOHN: It doesn't!

THERESA: Then I don't matter anymore?

JOHN: I didn't say that.

THERESA: And the kids.

JOHN: How, in the name a God, did you work that one out? My children do concern me. You concern me. This house concerns me ... very, very much. But—

THERESA: But what?

JOHN: I need to do what I'm doin' at the dock!

THERESA: That's just my point! You think more of that than you do of me and the children.

JOHN: Don't talk stupid!

THERESA: I'm not talkin' stupid and I've had enough. I've had it up to here of you!

JOHN: Do you think I'm havin' great fun? I'm just as sick of you as you are of me!

THERESA: Get out then!

JOHN: You get out! [*They both stand in acrimonious silence. Finally,* JOHN *speaks.*] Theresa. [*No reply*] Theresa. Just let me get on with it, will ya? [*Still no response*] I know it means you and the children sufferin'. But we will all benefit from it in the long run. I know what it means to you, but I could never answer to my conscience if I lived out thirty years at the dock in silence. Just to eke out the same miserable existence that m'da and all the other dockers have lived through. Only to retire early with a bad back, a bad chest and a weak heart. Theresa, I just couldn't do it. [*Silence*]

THERESA: I wouldn't want you to.

JOHN: What?

THERESA: I wouldn't want you to. I couldn't live with it myself. I'm sorry, I've been selfish.

[JOHN *goes over to her and puts his hands on her shoulders.*]

JOHN: No, you haven't.

THERESA: I have.

JOHN: You haven't. You were only doin' what you thought best for your children.

THERESA: And you.

JOHN: I know that. [*He turns* THERESA *round to face him.*]

THERESA: And anyway.

JOHN: Anyway what?

THERESA: I don't want to finish my days sittin' across the fire from an old, cantankerous, retired husband in bad health. [*They both smile.*]

JOHN: I can't guarantee you won't. Can you guarantee me that I won't end up bein' nagged to the grave by a silly, dotin' oul' woman?

THERESA: No, I can't.

JOHN: That makes it evens. [*They kiss.*]

THERESA: You will promise me one thing, John?

JOHN: What's that?

THERESA: That if you don't help to change things at the dock, say ... within a year or two, you'll get out before they hurt you?
[JOHN *breaks away.*]

JOHN: Don't be silly. No one's gonna hurt me.

THERESA: You know it can happen. It's happened to other people who said the wrong things.

JOHN: If it satisfies you any, yes, I'll get out if I don't make any realistic headway inside—how long did you give me?

THERESA: A year or two and no more.

JOHN: That's not very long ... but it's a deal. Right?

THERESA: Right, but—

JOHN: But, but, but! Will the said Theresa Graham, *née* McAllister, give the said Mr. John Joseph Graham, her fullest co-operation and understanding in his pursuit of better wages and conditions at the deep-sea docks in the borough and town of Belfast?

THERESA: I will, m'Lord.

JOHN: Case dismissed. [*They both laugh.*] Nigh, where the hell is that book.

THERESA: Right, I'll go round for the kids, then, before our Mary takes rickets.

JOHN: Don't be sittin' round there all day.

THERESA: Don't worry, I won't. I'm happy. In fact, I'll be dancin' on air all the way there and back.

JOHN: Watch the buses!

[THERESA *exits.* JOHN *goes on a thorough search of the room for the book. Presently, the door is rapped loudly and* JACK HENRY *and* MCKIBBEN *enter in an angry mood.*]

HENRY: What did you say to Jimmy Sweeney?

JOHN: What are you talkin' about?

MCKIBBEN: You know fine well what we're talkin' about. You threatened another member of our union a while ago.

JOHN: I what!

HENRY: That's right. We've been told you threatened Sweeney that you'd get him.

MCKIBBEN: For supposedly causin' an accident at a boat.

JOHN: That's a lie! I never threatened anybody. We did have words, yes.

HENRY: Words! You listen to me, Graham.

JOHN: No, you listen to me. For a start, you have no right to walk into the privacy of my home to brow-bate me. I never threatened anybody and I don't care whether you believe me or not.

MCKIBBEN: Don't push your luck, Graham, or I'll flatten you where you stand.

JOHN: You punchin' won't change my views. Give it a rest.

[MCKIBBEN *steps forward menacingly.*]

HENRY: Leave it! That won't be necessary ... yet! Nigh, listen, bucko, you're only—

JOHN: I told you, you've no right to—

HENRY: Listen! Shut up and listen for once! You're only on the committee a meal-hour. If you have any ambitions of stayin' on it, you're doin' all the wrong things.

MCKIBBEN: And shut your trap or I'll shut it for you.

JOHN: I spoke to Jimmy Sweeney about an accident at his boat. I am a committee man and—

HENRY: I don't wanna hear that nigh, but you better have a good explanation in the mornin'. [HENRY *and* MCKIBBEN *turn and walk to the exit.*]

JOHN: What is this? [*Both men stop.*] The Mafia?

HENRY: You'll see. [*They exit.*]

Black-out

ACT TWO

SCENE 1

The dockers enter by the schooling-pen. JIMMY SWEENEY *jumps up on the platform, while* JACK HENRY *stands to the side.*

LEG: Nothin's the same anymore, John, son. Young people want more out of life nigh. I don't know where it's all gonna end.

JOHN: Maybe it's just beginnin'.

LEG: God forbid. Hey, I wonder what Sweeney's at?

JOHN: No idea. [LEG *speaks to* SWEENEY *while* MCKIBBEN *looks down the road.*]

LEG: Dutch boat, John. C'mon, we'll stand in.

MCKIBBEN: Alright, away yiz go!

[*The men surge up against the barrier.*]

SWEENEY: Right! You! And you! Lindsay! Quinn! Murphy! You and you! [MCKIBBEN *moves to the front of the platform.*]

MCKIBBEN: Come on, lads, stand back.

SWEENEY: McKibben! And McNamara and that's it!

[SWEENEY *jumps down and exits with* HENRY. *As most of the dockers exit, the remaining few stand about chatting.* LEG *stops beside* JOHN *on his way out.*]

LEG: Jasis, I don't know how I got that. [*Looking at his disc*] He must be short of a man for over-the-hatch. [JOHN *shows little or no reaction.*] I'll a ... I'll get on down to this boat. I'll maybe see you later in Barney's.

JOHN: Yeah, sure Leg, see you in Barney's. [LEG *exits.* JOHN *stares blankly in front. Presently* SWEENEY *enters followed by* HENRY.]

SWEENEY: Right, yousens! I need two extra men to do a bit of loadin' in the Chapel sheds. [*The three remaining men walk forward, including* JOHN GRAHAM] Okay, you and you! That's it!

[SWEENEY *strides off.* GRAHAM *and* HENRY *exchange blunt stares, before* HENRY *walks off.* JOHN *stands disconsolate, before sitting down on the platform to read a newspaper. In a moment,* BUCKETS MCGUINNESS *enters, somewhat inebriated.*]

BUCKETS: Ah, young Graham, I thought for a while there I was late. Isn't it good to be early for a change. You know, us trade unionists, know like, us class-conscious types, we have to weigh in early and not give the bosses a chance to stick the boot in over time-keepin'. Like, if I dropped my high standards, they'd sack me as quick as the swally their Holy Communion. Is there ... is there something wrong? What ails ye?

JOHN: Ah, I'm alright, Buckets. Dead on, dead on.

BUCKETS: Here. [*Takes a bottle of wine from his inside pocket*] Take a wee drop of that. It'll liven you up, kid.

JOHN: No, you're alright, thanks. [BUCKETS *takes a drink himself.*]

BUCKETS: You know, it's marvellous what a drop of drink'll do for ye. When Churchill tuck a drink he fancied himself as a bricklayer. It's true. He built walls all over Downin' Street, blocked up doorways, windys, the lot. When he retired as prime minister, the had to employ demolition men to let them into 14 rooms. That's true. Every word of it. A sister of my cousin's brother-in-law used to work for him. Aye, you need to be either mad or drunk to get on in this world. Or both. That's why the Rasputins, the Hitlers and the Churchills got on so well. Whereas, if you're sober and sensitive, your brain's permanently wrapped in barbed-wire. And every time your emotion responds to what you see round ye, the barbed-wire sticks in hard. [*He takes a drink of wine.*] I'm neither sensitive nor sober and thank Thee, Lord, for this sweet life. [*He holds up the bottle towards the sky in jubilation.*] I'm havin' great fun. Hey! Where in the name a Jasis is everybody? It's not a holiday, is it? [*He sets the bottle down behind him.*]

JOHN: What?

BUCKETS: I said, where is everybody, where's the work?

JOHN: You're a bit late. Everybody's schooled and away to work n'all.

BUCKETS: I don't believe ye. What! That oul' clock of ours must be runnin' slow again. That means I'll have to spend another day in Barney's. Who was it decided that I should be brought into the world in Sailortown? Who was it decreed that m'own da should give me my first drink at 13 years of age? Why the hell amn't I a steady, chapel-goin' pillar of the community? Who was it picked me to be me? [*He picks up his bottle of wine only to find there is no wine left.*] Who was at m'bottle of blow?

JOHN: Nobody only yourself.

BUCKETS: Right, then, Barney's it is. Where are you for?

JOHN: Round to the canteen for a cup of tea before the union meetin'.

BUCKETS: Not workin'?

JOHN: Naa. Sweeney deliberately cut the ears off me.

BUCKETS: Shootin' your mouth off?

JOHN: Probably.

BUCKETS: Henry behind it?

JOHN: Probably. That's what this meetin's about. There's gonna be a row over what I'm supposed to have said to Sweeney. Imagine, it's gonna be me that's—

BUCKETS: Listen, listen, lis ... en! Never go round crabbin' cause you're gettin' the water cut outiv ye.

JOHN: I'm not crabbin'. I'm just sayin'. The union's puttin' the hammer on me so I'm goin' round here to squeal the place down.

BUCKETS: Watch that. Don't make the mistake of turnin' union activity into union wreckin'.

JOHN: But there's problems inside the union.

BUCKETS: And would you tell me what union hasn't got problems? Just never let that divert you from the real thing—the struggle with the employers. On every issue, luck to put the onus on the employers. They own you, me, the newspapers, the city, the dock, everything. Ownin' means responsibility. Don't take it off them for the wages they pay out.

JOHN: That's all easier said than done. If they won't face up to the employers, they'll have to face up to me. And if they want a row, I'll give them it.

BUCKETS: And who'll win?

JOHN: I don't care who wins. I'll let them know they've been in a fight.

BUCKETS: You're bate!

JOHN: What?

BUCKETS: You're bate before you start with that kind of talk. 'I don't care who wins.' That's the talk of a boxer who knows he's gonna take a dive before he gets into the ring.

JOHN: I didn't mean it like that. It's just that ... I'm gettin' frustrated ... fed-up.

BUCKETS: Stick it out, kid, stick it out. The future depends on you. You wouldn't like to think that in twenty years time, things were just as bad for the dockers, just because you got fed-up and made a pig's-arse of things. C'mon, we'll get away outta here. [*They walk towards the exit.*] Are you sure you weren't at this? [*Shakes the bottle*]

JOHN: For Jasis sake. [*They exit.*]

SCENE 2

BARNEY *is behind the bar of an otherwise empty public house.* SARAH
MONTAGUE *and* MARY-ANN MCKEOWN *enter.*

SARAH: I'm tired tellin' ye, tired tellin' ye! If he doesn't go out to
work, throw him out on his backside.

MARY-ANN: I wisht I had the heart to do it.

SARAH: You're very foolish, I wouldn't put up with it.

MARY-ANN: Sarah, it's alright you talkin', but I'm married to the man
nearly twenty years. I may see it out nigh.

SARAH: Bein' married to him doesn't mean you've to lift him and
lay him. You wanna catch yourself on.

MARY-ANN: Sure, if I didn't luck after him, he'd walk out and leave
me. He's done it before, as you well know.

SARAH: Aye, but you'd wee childer then. Yours is all grew up nigh.
Let him run on wherever the hell he likes.

MARY-ANN: But, sure, where would he get his grub? God knows the
trouble he'd get into on his own.

SARAH: I'm wastin' my time talkin' to you, wastin' my time. Do you
know what your trouble is, Mary-Ann McKeown? You're still
fond of him. That's your trouble. Still fond of him. Barney! Was
Buckets McGuinness in here yet? [BARNEY *appears unsure.*]

BARNEY: Oh a ... no ... no, I haven't saw him this mornin'.

SARAH: Just as I thought. He's hidin' from me. C'mon, missus, we'll
try the other one up at the corner. A frog never wanders far
from the water! [MARY-ANN *stands puzzled.*] What's wrong with ye
nigh?

MARY-ANN: I coulda swore I saw him comin' in here earlier on.

SARAH: That man of yours has ye away in the head. Are ye comin'?

MARY-ANN: Oh yes, Sarah, I'm comin' alright, I'm comin'. I've to get
the messages in for his dinner.

SARAH: Sometimes I wonder. Did you never think of gettin' him put
away in a home? That's what he needs. His arse well-warmed!
[*The two women exit chatting. From the other end of the bar,* BUCKETS
MCGUINNESS *enters from the toilets, doing up his fly. He walks across the
bar rather unsteadily and proceeds to go asleep at a table decorated with
various glasses and bottles of drink.* BARNEY *comes over to clear some of
the empty glasses at Buckets' table. He shakes* BUCKETS.]

BARNEY: Come on a that w'ye, man. Waken up! Your woman was in
here luckin' you.

BUCKETS: What! Where! You'd do what!

BARNEY: How did you get into that state? It's not even dinner-hour yet and you're stupid drunk.

BUCKETS: I don't drink. I mean ... I need a drink. Give is a wine.

BARNEY: Give you a wine! Sure, you can't even lift your chin to finish what's in front of you. Will I throw this out? [BUCKETS *shakes his head furiously.*] Well, you don't seem able to drink it, so what'll I do with it?

BUCKETS: Just ... throw it round me. [BARNEY *returns to the bar.*]

BARNEY: Oh, I shoulda known better than to waken a man up from the horrors of drink. You'd better get away outta here afore she comes back. [BUCKETS *makes his way to the bar.*]

BUCKETS: This drinkin's no good. I take far too much of the stuff. I'm definitely goin' round to St. Joseph's to take the pledge.

[SARAH MONTAGUE *enters. She throws* BARNEY *an accusing glance.*]

SARAH: Buckets McGuinness, where's my money?

BUCKETS: What money are you talkin' about?

SARAH: Don't you what money me. I want four pound eighteen shillins right this very minute.

BUCKETS: What? [*He looks round behind him*] Are you sure you've got the right person?

SARAH: As sure as every July has a Twelfth, I'm sure. C'mon. Where's the three pound you got to lift the suit out of the pawn?

BUCKETS: Oh! That money! [*Rummages through his pockets in pretence*] Why didn't you say it was that money? I haven't got it. But! But there's a spud boat due in this week and I'll definitely get a few days outiv it, Mrs. Montague, definitely.

SARAH: First, it was a timber boat, nigh it's a spud boat. Do you think I'm not wise?

BUCKETS: Of course, you're not ... I mean ... You're a wise oul' bastard, no I didn't mean that ... I meant my wife's an oul' bastard. Because, Mrs. Montague, I had every ha'penny I owed you in this trouser pocket last night afore I went to bed. But, like a dishonest Florence Nightingale, the bloody woman rifled m'pockets durin' the night, and left me with not even the price of five Woodbine. Nigh, would you credit that?

SARAH: I wouldn't credit anything concernin' you.

BUCKETS: Know what she wanted the money for? Food! To buy bloody food! What a waste of hard-earned money. I wisht I'd a woman that shared my interests in life.

SARAH: I do. Money! And I want it nigh!

BUCKETS: I haven't got it.

SARAH: Right, then, that definitely means trouble for you. That's the last you'll get and you know what that means. Send us in a wee gin, Barney. [*Exit* SARAH *to snug.*]

BUCKETS: What the hell am I gonna do nigh? That's the Bank a Monty Carlo well snookered.

BARNEY: That's your problem, if you wouldn't luck on a pound note as a drinkin' voucher, you'd be a bit better off.

BUCKETS: I've always said that.

BARNEY: Said what?

BUCKETS: I've always argued round this dock that the should pay us out in drinkin' vouchers.

BARNEY: That way, your wife'd never see a ha'penny.

BUCKETS: I can't get anybody to understand that. Anyway, I may try and get a few days work from somewhere this week. [*Enter* LEG] Here, Leg, is the spud boat in yet or do you know when it's due?

LEG: Are you on your geg? The spud boat pulled outta here for Cyprus dinner hour yesterday, cargo discharged an'all. If you hurry, you might catch it—off the coast of Portugal. [LEG *laughs.*]

BUCKETS: It's no laughin' matter, Leg. This oul' hure's luckin' her money an' I haven't a match.

LEG: As per usual. I may buy you another drink. Barney, a bottle a stout and a wine.

BUCKETS: No! No! I'm away, Leg. I have to go.

LEG: What! You're refusin' your medicine? That doesn't happen often.

BUCKETS: It's not often I owe her the guts of a fiver.

LEG: Well, where are you goin'?

BUCKETS: Where do you think? To luck for another moneylender to pay her back. [*Exit* BUCKETS.]

LEG: Well, Barney, how's things? Has any of the committee been in yet?

BARNEY: Not so bad, Leg. No a ... none of them's been in yet, but it's still early.

LEG: Aye, I suppose it is. I was up in the Union Rooms with the young lad payin' his fee. I'm just waitin' on the committee endorsin' his name.

BARNEY: I was glad to see Danny-boy gettin' his button. He's a hell of a nice kid. But you want to keep him away from that fella that just walked out there or he'll end up the same way as many another young fella that went round the dock. Bad company, bad habits and afore you know it, Skid Row. It's alright bein' a coat-puller at Bucket McGuinness' age, but when you luck at some a the young men, you'd wonder what has them the way they are.

LEG: The casual system, Barney. One week you're like Paul Getty and the next you're bummin' it. I'll have to watch the lad. But, then again, it won't be long till he's married and I'll have no say in the matter. He'll have his own life to lead then. But I think he's sensible enough. He'll luck after thon wee girl well. Sure the were up luckin' at a house there last week and I think they're gonna buy it.

BARNEY: And it's not many can buy a house afore they're married.

LEG: 'Tis not. But she's workin' and with him gettin' a button and that, they've everything planned. The two a them, God spares them, 'll be married afore Christmas. [*Enter* JOHN GRAHAM] Ach, billy John, how'd the meetin' go?

JOHN: It didn't go. Give is a beer, Barney.

LEG: What do you mean?

JOHN: I mean there was trouble.

LEG: Why, what happened?

JOHN: They put me on trial over Danny-boy's accident. It wasn't *how* did this accident happen, it was *why* did you threaten Jimmy Sweeney.

LEG: What did you say?

JOHN: I proposed that Jimmy Sweeney, as foreman of that boat, should be suspended pendin' an inquiry into how there was 13 begs in the heaves. Jasis, they near ate me!

LEG: And didn't accept it?

JOHN: Didn't accept it? All hell broke loose and it ended up with me callin' McKibben a lickspittle and walkin' out. Leg, I'm not luckin' for trouble but I really think I had no alternative.

LEG: Oh, it's gonna be blood and snatters from here on in. And you saw the way Sweeney left you standin' in the pen this mornin'. How or why he picked me, I don't know. Tell is, was Danny-boy's name cleared for the union?

JOHN: It was, aye. His and another ten were cleared.

LEG: That's great. Danny-boy'll be pleased to hear that. But where does that leave you, John?

JOHN: Disgusted with the whole bloody lot of them.

LEG: Are you gonna pack it in?

JOHN: I don't know. I'm fightin' a lone battle. I need more support.

LEG: And how are you gonna get that?

JOHN: Well, the May Day march is comin' up this Saturday and if I can get as many dockers to that as possible, it'll maybe reawaken something in them.

LEG: There's never many usually turns out for it, John.

JOHN: Don't I know. They'd rather march in their hundreds on St. Patrick's Day, commemeratin' a friggin' myth, than march as part of the workin'-class movement through the streets of their own city. It's the same old story in Ireland. Socialism versus the Saints. And here we are, the only Third World country in western Europe, and the Saints is winnin' hands down. Will you be there yourself?

LEG: Ah God, Jasis, no, John. I couldn't march with my leg. But I never used to miss it years ago. You'll have some trouble gettin' McKibben and company there. [HUGHIE *and* DANNY-BOY *enter. Danny-boy's arm is in a sling.*] Oh luck what the wind blew in. Is that boat finished?

HUGHIE: Aye, I got away early. There was only two hundred ton in it. So I thought I'd go up and take Danny-boy out for a drink.

JOHN: How's the arm?

DANNY-BOY: A wee bit sore, but I'll live.

JOHN: You were lucky. By the way, you're in the union.

HUGHIE: Heyyyyyy! [*Slaps* DANNY-BOY *on the back*] No problem, our kid. You're made nigh.

DANNY-BOY: That's great. I think that calls for a celebration. Da, buy is a drink?

LEG: I knew that was comin'. Barney, two bottles a beer.

JOHN: Well, son, how does it feel to be a fully-fledged member of the union?

DANNY-BOY: Terrific. I just hope the work comes along.

HUGHIE: It better come along. Danny-boy needs every penny he can earn.

JOHN: So do we all.

HUGHIE: Aye, but Danny-boy needs money quick, don't you, D-B? Tell them.

LEG: Tell is what? [DANNY-BOY *is embarrassed.*]

HUGHIE: Tell them, Danny.

LEG: Well?

DANNY-BOY: I'm bringing the weddin' forward, da.

LEG: Forward? When to?

DANNY-BOY: Very soon.

LEG: How soon?

DANNY-BOY: Not this Saturday, but next! Susan's expectin'. She's due in a coupla months.

LEG: Holy Christ!

HUGHIE: Isn't that great, da?

LEG: Aye, great—I mean no, no!

HUGHIE: That's what we called in here for. We were wantin' to see you, Barney, about bookin' upstairs for the reception?

BARNEY: No problem. It's there for yiz.

LEG: Does your mother know about this?

DANNY-BOY: Yeah, she knows all about it.

HUGHIE: There was a wee bit of blurtin' and cryin' but she came round in the end and we all had a good laugh. [*Enter* MARY-ANN MCKEOWN *from the street.*] Da, it's no use askin' any more questions. Danny-boy's girl's pregnant and he has to get married quick. And that's all about it.

[MARY-ANN *lets out a squeal and rushes towards the snug.*]

MARY-ANN: Sarah! Sarah! Do you hear that? Sarah! [*As she disappears into the snug, her voice is heard. The others gape after her in bewilderment.*] God, Sarah, did you hear that? Are you not listenin' to what's goin' on round ye?

SARAH: What ails ye, woman?

MARY-ANN: That young fella McNamara has some wee girl in the family way and has to marry her. They're standin' out there talkin' about it right nigh. [*Enter* SARAH *and* MARY-ANN.]

SARAH: Right, which one of yiz done it?

HUGHIE: It's our Danny-boy here, Mrs. Montague. He's blowin' the fuse.

SARAH: He's what?

HUGHIE: Gettin' happily harried, know?

SARAH: Oh, he is, is he? And is this right about the wee girl bein' pregnant?

HUGHIE: Dead right. Maybe twins.

SARAH: Where's she from?

DANNY-BOY: Limestone Road

SARAH: Do you mean she's a Protestant?

DANNY-BOY: Church of Ireland.

MARY-ANN: God love and protect is.

SARAH: Are you turnin'?

DANNY-BOY: I don't know yet.

LEG: He won't be.

SARAH: Nobody's talkin' to you. When's the weddin'?

DANNY-BOY: Saturday week.

SARAH: You'd need to make up your mind, son. Have you even decided what the childer's gonna be?

HUGHIE: Some a them might be girls and some a them might be boys. [*Laughter*]

SARAH: What are you laughin' at, greasy hair? A dacent girl wouldn't venture near you for a kiss, never mind to get pregnant. [*They all laugh except* HUGHIE *and* SARAH.] Well, whoever gets married these days needs luck and you'll need all you can get. Give the boys a drink, Barney.

[*The men all cheer.* SARAH *pays and walks towards the snug with* MARY-ANN. DANNY-BOY *calls after her.*]

DANNY-BOY: Oh, thanks very much, Mrs. Montague, that was very nice of you. I was wonderin', Mrs. Montague, if you would do me a wee favour. I'm not luckin' the loan a money nigh. Just ... just a wee favour between you and me.

MARY-ANN: Maybe he wants you to do Matron of Honour, Sarah.

SARAH: Would you like to mind your own business?

MARY-ANN: Whatever you like nigh, Sarah, it's all the same to me.

DANNY-BOY: No, I wondered if you would, as a special favour for me gettin' married, like, a sort of weddin' present, would you not give Buckets McGuinness a bit more time to pay back the money he owes you?

SARAH: Have you been drinkin' wine?

LEG: Ach, go on Sarah. It'll do you no harm.

HUGHIE: C'mon a that w'ye.

SARAH: Not a chance!

JOHN: Do it for Danny-boy.

MARY-ANN: Maybe you should, Sarah. He's not a bad oul' crater.

DANNY-BOY: Just this once, Mrs. Montague. Poor oul' Buckets. He's runnin' round distracted about it. Just a couple of weeks?

[SARAH *turns and walks towards the snug.*]

SARAH: He doesn't deserve it. You can tell him, for I'm not.

DANNY-BOY: Thanks, thanks, Mrs. Montague. [*The two women exit to the snug.*]

BARNEY: If I hadna saw it with my own eyes, I wouldn't believe it. First, she buys the bar a drink and then she reprieves Buckets McGuinness. She couldn't be well.

JOHN: Stranger things have happened.

LEG: Here, I'm away back to work. Put that one over for me, Barney. I'm over the hatch for this man Sweeney and you daren't be late.

JOHN: Right, Leg, see you later on.

HUGHIE: See ya, da.

[LEG *moves towards exit.* DANNY-BOY *moves after him.*]

DANNY-BOY: Da! Da, you're not against me gettin' married, are ye? Like, you're not annoyed or anything?

LEG: What age are you nigh, Danny-boy?

DANNY-BOY: Twenty-two.

LEG: For Jasis sake, I was married with two childer by the time I was 22. Of course, I'm not annoyed. [*He puts his arm around Danny-boy's shoulder.*] In fact, me and your mother'll do all we can to put the weddin' over. You can depend on that. Thon's a nice wee girl you have. Luck after her. I'll see yiz later.

DANNY-BOY: See ya, da. [LEG *exits.*]

BARNEY: Listen, John, I'm away upstairs for a minute or two. Give is a shout if somebody comes in.

JOHN: Work away, Barney. [BARNEY *exits.*] Right. Nigh that I've got you two men together, what about the May Day parade on Saturday? Are yiz marchin'?

DANNY-BOY: What parade?

JOHN: The May Day parade.

HUGHIE: What time's it at, John?

JOHN: Eleven a'clock.

DANNY-BOY: When did you say it was?

HUGHIE: Saturday, ya ejit ye!

DANNY-BOY: And what's it for?

JOHN: It's what's known as International Workers' Day. It's the day when workers from all over the world march through their towns and cities in solidarity with the cause of Labour and the trade union movement.

HUGHIE: I couldn'ta put it better myself.

JOHN: While we're marchin' through Belfast, we know that thousands, in fact millions of men and women are walkin' through the streets of London, New York, Moscow, Paris, Madrid, you name it. That's the day the organised workin'-class is on the march.

HUGHIE: Organised is right!

JOHN: This year we're tryin' to get as many dockers as possible to turn out.

DANNY-BOY: Well, I definitely couldn't go on it. M'da has me lined up for a job with Sweeney, workin' the weekend. Like, I have to weigh in. I need the money badly.

HUGHIE: I'm workin' the weekend, too, but I've arranged to get away on Saturday mornin' for the march and get back to the boat as soon as it's finished. And then I've to get away to the Plaza that night.

DANNY-BOY: Aye, but you're not workin' with Jimmy Sweeney.

HUGHIE: I'm in the next hatch with McKenna and he's as bad. I just told him straight, I was goin' to the march.

JOHN: I don't think Danny-boy's in a position to rear up at any boss with him just into the union, Hughie. It's the casual system round here, remember?

HUGHIE: Well, nigh that you mention it. I read an article in the paper the other day about some of the unions in England talkin' about scrubbin' the casual system and askin' for a guaranteed fall-back pay when there's no work in.

JOHN: Yeah, I read that myself and the sooner the better. This casual system round here is unique within organised labour.

HUGHIE: It's ancient.

DANNY-BOY: What's wrong with it?

JOHN: Don't tell me, Danny-boy, you see nothin' wrong with what goes on in that schoolin' pen every mornin'. Grown up men shovin' and pushin' each other for whatever's goin'.

DANNY-BOY: That's the way it's organised.

JOHN: That's not organised life, Danny, that's anarchy. The strongest survive, the weakest go to the wall. It's anarchy alright, but you won't hear their mouthpieces puttin' it over like that. No, they use words like hard work, endeavour, enterprise, initiative.

HUGHIE: Too right. Educated bastards. That's what's wrong with us, we're not educated enough to twist big words and meanins round to suit ourselves. Like the merchants the pour out of Oxford and Cambridge.

JOHN: Yeah, it's a nice wee set-up, isn't it? Do you know that almost every single Cabinet since the war has been made up of these Oxford and Cambridge characters?

HUGHIE: Aye, what chance had we got, goin' to Earl Street school?

JOHN: That's it, Hughie, the dice are stacked against ye, even before you're born.

DANNY-BOY: Because of where you're born?

JOHN: Definitely. We'll never have an influence in government and it all starts with the education set-up.

HUGHIE: If we did, there'd be changes. The Plaza wouldn't be so dear for a start. There'd be changes alright.

JOHN: And since the people who go to Oxford and Cambridge come from the middle and upper classes, try and guess what side they'll be on when they get into government?

DANNY-BOY: All's I wanna be's a docker.

HUGHIE: You're wastin' your time, John. He's as thick as two short planks. D-B, do you know that John's been gettin' into rows over your accident?

JOHN: We'll just have to wait on him findin' out for himself.

[BUCKETS MCGUINNESS *enters. He appears to be not in such a good mood.*]

DANNY-BOY: Ach, there you are nigh, Buckets. Where were you?

[BUCKETS *is silent.*]

JOHN: Ah, the boul' Buckets doesn't luck in the best of form. I better get offside before he starts throwin' punches. I'm away down to the canteen to drum up some support for the march. See yiz later, lads. Y'alright, Buckets? [JOHN *laughs as he exits.*]

DANNY-BOY: Buckets, what's wrong with ya? Hey, we've got good news for you.

BUCKETS: What? Sarah Montague's been run over be a bus?

HUGHIE: Even better.

BUCKETS: What? The bus reversed back over her again?

DANNY-BOY: I'm tellin' ye, Buckets, all your troubles are over.

BUCKETS: You mean the wife's dead?

HUGHIE: No. Danny-boy worked the article for ye. You'll be a happy man when you hear this story.

BUCKETS: I couldn't for the life a me listen to any wee stories. I'm not in the form for it. I musta been knocked back by every moneylender in Belfast the day.

DANNY-BOY: Where were you?

BUCKETS: Where wasn't a? I was all round Sailortown, York Street, up the Falls, the Shankill. I even ended up in the City Hall.

HUGHIE: What were you doin' in the City Hall?

BUCKETS: Tryin' to register m'self as a charity. [BUCKETS *takes a glass and leans over the counter, helping himself to some wine.*]

DANNY-BOY: And what'd the Lord Mayor say?

BUCKETS: He wasn't bad about it. Very understandin'. He says, 'Buckets, I've known you a long time.'

DANNY-BOY: You mean you know the Lord Mayor of Belfast?

BUCKETS: Know him? Me and him has a long association together with a very worthy charity. Dr. Barnardo's Home.

HUGHIE: How's that?

BUCKETS: He was Honorary President and I was reared in it. And I'm tellin' ye I was down seein' him and he was very understandin' about it. He takes me out to the front door, away from the other councillors, and he says to me, 'Buckets, I've known you a long time and you know me, right?' I says, 'That's right, Mr. Lord Mayor, you know me well, very well indeed.' He says, 'I know I do. Nigh fuck off outta here afore I get you arrested.' [HUGHIE *and* DANNY-BOY *laugh.*] The cheek a him. Jasis, I mind him when he only owned one shop!

DANNY-BOY: But, listen, we were talkin' to Sarah Montague.

BUCKETS: Fraternisin' with the enemy? The shot men like you in the last war.

HUGHIE: It concerns you, Buckets.

BUCKETS: Luck, I don't wanna hear nothin' about that oul' embezzler the day. I'm just about sick hearin' the woman's name. [SARAH MONTAGUE *enters.*] And I couldn't care less about her or her few shillins. It was only happens when I was able to work down the houl' of a boat.

SARAH: What's that about my money?

BUCKETS: I said, bollocks you and your money, you oul' hurebeg! You'd think I was goin' to run outta the country to see you. What?

SARAH: And I thought I was doin' you a good turn.

BUCKETS: Doin' who a good turn? At five shillins in the pound, that's daylight robbery. [HUGHIE *and* DANNY-BOY *are embarrassed.*]

SARAH: Four pound, eighteen shillins. I want it for Saturday. Every brown penny! [SARAH *storms out of the bar.* BUCKETS *shouts after her.*]

BUCKETS: You've some chance!

DANNY-BOY: Buckets!

HUGHIE: You've got it all wrong!

BUCKETS: I'd go to jail first. What! Dick Turpin wore a mask!

DANNY-BOY: Buckets! I spoke to her the day and she agreed to give you another two weeks to clear your slate.

BUCKETS: You'll not make little outta me! Who! Four pound, eighteen shillins didn't rear me! What did you say?

DANNY-BOY: Will you for frig sake listen! We all spoke to Mrs. Montague on your behalf and she agreed to let the money go for a while.

HUGHIE: A few weeks, she said.

BUCKETS: Ah Jasis! I don't believe yiz.

DANNY-BOY: Frig, that's what we were tryin' to tell you all along.

HUGHIE: But you wouldn't listen.

BUCKETS: Why me? Why was I out kickin' futball when the brains was bein' given out?

SCENE 3

The Graham home. THERESA *is putting on her coat and scarf and is about to leave. She looks for her shopping bag.* JOHN *enters.*

THERESA: No work this mornin'?

JOHN: None.

THERESA: Oh, before I forget. M'mammy wants us to go to her house on Saturday and to start the wallpaperin'.

JOHN: Does she?

THERESA: She has the wallpaper in a fortnight nigh and you know she's nobody to do it for her.

JOHN: Sure thon place isn't worth paperin'. It's fallin' down round her.

THERESA: She does her best.

JOHN: And anyway, I'll be at the May Day march on Saturday.

THERESA: Ach, John.

JOHN: Make it the following weekend.

THERESA: Saturday and Sunday?

JOHN: Saturday and Sunday.

THERESA: That's good. I'll call in and let her know.

JOHN: What about some dinner, missus?

THERESA: I'm goin'. I'll not be long. If Eamonn comes in out of school give him a plate of cornflakes till I get back. I'm away ... Oh, here. Do you know what he said to me this mornin' as I was puttin' him out to school?

JOHN: No, what?

THERESA: He said when he grows up, he's goin' to be a schoolteacher.

JOHN: A schoolteacher! What put that into his head?

THERESA: I've no idea, but he seems to like school. Very good at doin' his homework and that.

JOHN: But a schoolteacher?

THERESA: John, I'd love our Eamonn to stay on at school and become a schoolteacher.

JOHN: Theresa, he's only ten years of age. It's early yet.

THERESA: But why can't he?

JOHN: There's ... there's a whole lot of reasons. There's the 11-plus for a start. He has to pass that. And anyway, as he gets older he'll feel out of it, if he's the only one of his mates still studyin', while they all go on to the dock, or go to sea or something.

THERESA: Or the bru! Whatever happens, I don't want him to go to the dock.

JOHN: At the end of the day, that might be all there is.

THERESA: It won't be. I'm gonna make sure he gets as good an education as there is goin'.

JOHN: Aye, the same as you got. You can't even spell Dick and Dora. [JOHN *laughs.*]

THERESA: At least my head isn't buried in books all the time. And anyway, our teacher told us at school that we would get married and have babies.

JOHN: And am I sorry you tuck her advice.

THERESA: Huh! I don't know where you'd be the day without me. You hadn't an arse in your trousers till you married me.

[*The door is knocked and* HUGHIE MCNAMARA *enters.*]

HUGHIE: I hope I'm not interruptin' nothin'.

JOHN: Not a'tall, Hughie, come on in.

THERESA: No, come on in, Hughie McNamara. Get yourself well up to the fire there and put your feet up along with King Farouke. It's a man's life alright.

JOHN: That's what you'd like us to think. I'll get you a start on a beg-boat this week nigh, if you want. [*Both men laugh.*]

THERESA: Tell is this, Hughie, did you make it up with Sheila McKenna for the dancin' competition on Saturday night?

HUGHIE: It's all arranged.

THERESA: And?

HUGHIE: I'm partnerin' Connie Francis and I fixed *her* up with Buckets McGuinness!

THERESA: Funny.

HUGHIE: No, I'm only sleggin'. I've agreed to dance with her on one condition. That she just has to wreck m'hair once and I'm walkin' off the floor. [*He checks with his hand to make sure his hair is in place.*]

THERESA: I'm glad to hear that. Make sure you pay her in.

HUGHIE: Are you mad? Her da ownin' the newspaper stand in Royal Avenue and you want *me* to pay *her* in? I'll meet her inside as usual.

THERESA: And you're all set to win then?

HUGHIE: Not as confident as I would be if you were partnerin' me.

THERESA: No chance. But, you know, I think I would like to go to a dance one of these days.

HUGHIE: Throwin' hints, John.

JOHN: I never heard a word.

THERESA: No, seriously. I miss them days. Gettin' all done up for the dances. The make-up, the hair-dos, high-heels and everything.

And the fun we had when a crowd of us went into the town together. The butterflies and the whole atmosphere. It used to be great. I do miss them days. Especially the dancin'. I used to love dancin' with Miser O'Hare. He could really dance.

JOHN: If you really want, maybe we could go and watch Hughie on Saturday night.

THERESA: Yeah, maybe we should. Cheer him on.

HUGHIE: Fancy a swing nigh?

THERESA: What?

HUGHIE: Put me through m'paces for the competition? That's a great idea. C'mon.

THERESA: You couldn't dance here, Hughie, it's too ... [*She looks at* JOHN *apprehensively.*]

JOHN: Yiz might as well. Yiz are both mad.

HUGHIE: Right, c'mon girl, let's have ye. Put on a record there. [JOHN *and* HUGHIE *clear a dancefloor.*]

THERESA: And I have just the record for you, Hughie. [THERESA *is at the record-player.*]

HUGHIE: What is it?

THERESA: Wait'll ya hear. [*Music starts*] 'Stupid Cupid'!

HUGHIE: Connie Francis! [HUGHIE *and* THERESA *then go through a flashy jiving routine, cheered on by* JOHN. *At the end of it,* THERESA *flops on to a chair exhausted.*]

THERESA: Oh, that's enough for me. I'm not able for it anymore. I'm out of breath. [JOHN *and* HUGHIE *replace the furniture.*]

JOHN: Very good. That was first class.

HUGHIE: I never even got warmed up.

THERESA: Nobody'd believe it. Wait'll I tell m'ma that I was jivin' with Hughie McNamara in the middle of the kitchen, in the middle of the afternoon.

HUGHIE: Make sure and tell her your husband was here.

THERESA: Don't worry, she might think I'm mad but she definitely knows I'm not blind.

HUGHIE: Cheek! [*They all laugh as* THERESA *exits.*]

JOHN: Well, Hughie, you seem to be in top form for Saturday night.

HUGHIE: Book me, man, book me!

JOHN: What?

HUGHIE: Give me the message, book me. *The Ragged Trousered* thing. What do you think I came round here for? The book!

JOHN: Oh, I have it waitin' on ye.

HUGHIE: It's about time.

JOHN: There you are.

HUGHIE: Nigh, wait'll I tell you what I have for you.

JOHN: What? A brand new hook for the one you broke on me?

HUGHIE: No! A brand new book on Elvis! John, It's a cracker. Tons of photos. Photos that have never been printed before. You know, in the army and that. I haven't finished it yet, but you're the first one that's gettin' it after me.

JOHN: I can't wait.

HUGHIE: I knew you'd like it, John. Nigh. Another wee thing just as important I have to tell you.

JOHN: You're full of news the day.

HUGHIE: Well, I wanted to let you know that me and our Danny-boy have been talkin' about the whole union thing and we have decided to give you our full backin'.

JOHN: I thought I had that already.

HUGHIE: Aye. [*He clenches his fist.*] But we're talkin' about that!

JOHN: What?

HUGHIE: Don't be lettin' on to be stupid, John. We've worked it out that the way things is goin' up to nigh, these guys is gonna give you the push to get you outta the way.

JOHN: That's nonsense, Hughie.

HUGHIE: A wee bit of rough stuff's never happened before, like?

JOHN: Maybe in the old days. Luck, Hughie, I know what they're up to. But the threat of Harry McKibben doesn't scare me, and that's all it is at the moment—a threat.

HUGHIE: Well, let's meet threats with threats. Just to let them know you're not on your own. I've been in one or two rows before and with our D-B and yourself, we'll let them know what the score is.

JOHN: Hughie. Wait a minute. You've got it all wrong. I don't want to fight with anybody. I'm not scared of anybody, but that's just not the way I wanna go about things. I think I can win by fair argument and persuasion.

HUGHIE: That's too airy-fairy.

JOHN: Maybe so, but that's me. Good or bad, that's me.

HUGHIE: Do you think I couldn't handle McKibben?

JOHN: I'm sure you could. But I think I can handle him, too. Within the confines of the union.

HUGHIE: Are you sure?

JOHN: Definitely. I appreciate your offer, Hughie, but if there's gonna be any skulduggery, and I honestly don't think there will be, let it come from them. Let the dockers see them for what they are.

HUGHIE: But the dockers know them for what they are and none of them wants to do anything about it. M'own da's the biggest lickspittle goin'.

JOHN: It's only his way of survivin'.

HUGHIE: He shouldn't grovel.

JOHN: I don't blame him for grovellin'. The older men are hooked. We need to luck towards the younger lads comin' into the union, like your Danny-boy. That's where the changes'll come.

HUGHIE: That's probably why they're so reluctant to open the union books.

JOHN: That's part of it.

HUGHIE: I don't suppose I'll ever make the union nigh.

JOHN: You never know. We're into the sixties nigh. The economy's on the way up and if the union and the employers push for the proper development of Belfast Port, then with all the increased trade, the should be needin' a lot more dockers.

HUGHIE: But will that happen?

JOHN: Time will tell. In twenty years time, we'll be able to luck back and judge. In the meantime, McNamara, make sure you're out of your pit on Saturday mornin' for the march.

HUGHIE: You've a cheek. I was the first—[*There is a loud rap on the door.* JACK HENRY *and* MCKIBBEN *immediately enter.*]

HENRY: I'm here to notify you that, as a result of your behaviour at the meetin' today, you are suspended from the union committee until further notice.

JOHN: You have no right to do that.

HENRY: I have every right.

JOHN: Does that include invadin' the privacy of my home?

HENRY: We couldn't find you anywhere else.

JOHN: Well, I'd prefer if you didn't come here and I thought we'd already agreed on that.

HENRY: You had to be notified.

JOHN: Was my suspension passed by the whole committee?

HENRY: It was passed by me and that's enough.

JOHN: I'll check that in a union rule book.

HENRY: There are no union rule books.

JOHN: I'll get one from head office.

MCKIBBEN: Keep your nose outta head office or I'll knock it off.

HUGHIE: Would you like to try it?

JOHN: Hughie!

MCKIBBEN: What's this got to do with you, McNamara?

HUGHIE: Plenty.

JOHN: Hughie, I warned you to stay out of this.

HENRY: Union affairs don't concern you.

HUGHIE: My brother's accident concerns me and youse should be doin' something about it.

HENRY: It was his own fault.

HUGHIE: Ballicks!

MCKIBBEN: Keep that up, McNamara, and you're only markin' your own card.

HENRY: Alright, leave it. He doesn't concern us. But you do, Graham. You'll receive notification of my decision in writin' and you'll be asked to appear in front of the next committee meetin'. In the meantime, keep your mouth shut.

MCKIBBEN: Or I'll shut it for you.

HUGHIE: You'll not do it with your mouth.

JOHN: That's enough, Hughie. I told you I don't want things done that way.

HUGHIE: Sure they've suspended you.

JOHN: I'll deal with that. That's my problem.

HENRY: I'm glad you're showin' some respect, Graham.

JOHN: Common sense, Jack.

HENRY: I'll see you at the meetin'. [THERESA GRAHAM *enters.*]

THERESA: Oh, John, did you ... see ... sorry, I didn't realise there was anybody here.

HENRY: We were just goin'. [*The two union men exit.*]

JOHN: Nobody'll believe it.

THERESA: Believe what? What were they doin' at my door?

JOHN: Suspendin' me from the committee.

THERESA: What?

JOHN: Who would believe that our union does its business through illegal suspensions and physical threats to its members?

THERESA: You're suspended? What for?

JOHN: Forget it.

HUGHIE: For bein' a real shop steward, that's what for.

JOHN: Hughie, you let me down there. You know Jack Henry'll use that against me.

HUGHIE: Use what?

JOHN: He'll accuse me of havin' henchmen.

HUGHIE: But he's walked around with henchmen for 15 years.

JOHN: That's not the point.

THERESA: John Graham, I want you to tell me what exactly's goin' on here?

JOHN: I told you, it doesn't matter.

THERESA: It does matter. We've talked all this out, remember? What happened, Hughie?

HUGHIE: Oh, I was just headin' off, Theresa. It's not for me to say anything, one way or the other. I'll see you later, John.

JOHN: Aye. Oh, here, Hughie. Don't be walkin' out without your book.

HUGHIE: I near forgot that! I'll see yiz. [HUGHIE *exits.*]

THERESA: Well?

JOHN: Well what?

THERESA: What happened here? What did you mean when you said physical threats? Harry McKibben?

JOHN: That's nothin'.

THERESA: No, that's nothin'. He'll just beat you to a pulp one of these days, but that's nothin'.

JOHN: Luck, I thought we'd already agreed to let me get on in peace with union affairs?

THERESA: Yeah, but we also agreed that, if things went wrong, you'd get out.

JOHN: It's not that bad yet.

THERESA: No, it's just terrific. Harry McKibben's—

JOHN: Will you give over about Harry McKibben! Nigh, let's get this straight. What I do at the dock is my business. You stay out of it!

THERESA: I'm your wife! How can I stay out of it, even if I wanted to?

JOHN: 'Cause I'm tellin' you to.

THERESA: And I'm supposed to stand around passively while they break you in two?

JOHN: I told you. Nobody's gonna break me in two. I can handle it. Just leave me alone!

THERESA: You're not on your own to be left alone. You've a wife and two children in there somewhere.

JOHN: Don't make it any harder.

THERESA: I'm not. I'm just lettin' you know that you've more than yourself to think about.

JOHN: You're goin' over old ground.

THERESA: I need to. What about all that talk over Eamonn's education? What's he gonna do if his father ends up punch-drunk and broken? Or worse?

JOHN: For the last time, I'm doin' this for the children. It's so that we can be in a better financial situation to help with Eamonn's education.

THERESA: John, you're all fancy talk. Big ideas. The future! Someday! What about nigh!

JOHN: What about nigh?

THERESA: That's what I'm askin'.

JOHN: Don't you ever give over? Can I not get a wee bit of peace in my own house?

THERESA: It's not a matter of that.

JOHN: What is it a matter of?

THERESA: Talkin'.

JOHN: I'm fed up talkin'. [*He grabs his coat.*]

THERESA: We don't talk enough.

JOHN: I think we do. [*He moves towards exit.*]

THERESA: Where are you goin'?

JOHN: Timbucktoo! [*He exits.* THERESA *looks distressed.*]

SCENE 4

BARNEY *is flicking through a newspaper at the bar of his empty public house. Presently, the pub door opens and* BUCKETS MCGUINNESS *sticks his head inside.*

BUCKETS: Psst! Psst! Barney! [BARNEY *looks over.*] Is Sarah Montague here?

BARNEY: No, the coast is clear. [BUCKETS *enters.*]

BUCKETS: Thank God for that. You know, it's gettin' out of order. Give is a wine, Barney. There's not a pub in the whole a Sailortown I can have a peaceful drink in without havin' to luck over my shoulder for moneylenders.

BARNEY: It's you that borrowed the money.

BUCKETS: Unfortunately.

BARNEY: Maybe, someday, they'll go out of fashion.

BUCKETS: It couldn't come soon enough. I don't think it'll be too long afore hire purchase takes over from your backstreet moneylenders as the saviour of the workin'-class.

BARNEY: Do you think so?

BUCKETS: Jasis, I remember the day our neighbourhood first discovered hire purchase. Buck Alec, I think it was, who first caught on to the fact that you could get a brand new wireless outta one of the big shops downtown for one and thruppence.

BARNEY: Was that not only the deposit?

BUCKETS: And that was all the got. Boy, our district didn't half liven up. When you walked down the street, the doors and windys were lyin' wide open to the world with the latest music blarin' at top volume.

BARNEY: What did the shops do when nobody made any more payments?

BUCKETS: Ah, God, it was terrible. Would you believe me that within month the whole district was like a morgue. The shop came out with the peelers and tuck the whole lot back. I don't think the war was a bigger shock.

BARNEY: Well, tell me this and tell me no more. Did you square up that money for Sarah?

BUCKETS: As from here and nigh, I've decided I'm givin' her nothin'. Not a light is she gettin' a me.

BARNEY: You'll not get away with it.

BUCKETS: You know, Barney, everything in life has its advantages and disadvantages. Every single thing. Her advantage as a moneylender is the interest she charges. Her disadvantage is men like me not payin' her back.

BARNEY: I don't care what you say, when she comes through that door, you'll be expected to pay up. She only give you to Saturday and that's today.

BUCKETS: It's as good a day as any for it.

BARNEY: For what?

BUCKETS: For kickin' Sarah Montague's teeth down her throat. [*Enter* SARAH *and* MARY-ANN *from the street.*] And hittin' her a good boot up the arse! [BUCKETS *sees* SARAH *enter. He quickly swings round facing her.*] Ach, the very woman I want to see. [SARAH *stops and holds out her hand.*] That's what I've come to tell you about, Sarah, Mrs. Montague. I've something to tell you about that.

MARY-ANN: He's at it again, Sarah.

BUCKETS [*at* MARY-ANN, *speaking softly*]: I'm speakin' to Mrs. Montague. About the four pounds, eighteen shillins.

SARAH: No abouts!

BUCKETS: Will you listen to me, missus. It's about your oul' lad.

SARAH: What? What about Sam Montague?

BUCKETS: If you'll only listen to me for a minute, I'll tell ye. Nigh, this'll come as a surprise to you. Do you wanna sit down?

SARAH: Hurry up!

BUCKETS: Well, I was drinkin' with your husband last night in the White Lion. Nigh, afore I go any further, I'm gonna ask you a question. Did your oul' fella come in with an overcoat on last night or did he not?

SARAH: What of it?

MARY-ANN: He's only tryin' to get away from the point, Sarah.

BUCKETS: Would you kindly refrain from interrupting, Mary-Ann McKeown. Nigh, was the coat not brand new and did it have the name of a Dutch tailors on the inside?

SARAH: What's all this got to do with the money you owe me?

BUCKETS: That, Mrs. Montague, is precisely the point. I don't owe you anything. You owe me money.

SARAH: What?

MARY-ANN: I told you, Sarah. You shouldn't have listened to him.

BUCKETS: Go you and bollocks yourself! You see, I touched for that overcoat at the Dutch boat yesterday and sold it to your Sam for six quid and he told me to get the price of it of you. Nigh, I hated sums at school, but if you take the money I owe you away from the price of the coat, you owe me one pound two shillins, I think.

MARY-ANN: Oh my God, Sarah! [SARAH *stands in stunned silence.*]

BUCKETS: I'm not in any hurry for it, mind you. You'll have plenty of time to pay it since me and you has a long-standin' business arrangement. And no interest whatsoever.

MARY-ANN: What are you gonna do, Sarah? Are you gonna pay him?

BUCKETS: Take your time, Mrs. Montague, as I said. I'm fairly strong at the minute and I can wait for it.

SARAH: C'mon, Mary-Ann, I may go round and see this oul' gabshite. Are ya comin'?

MARY-ANN: Whatever you like nigh, Sarah. It's all the same to me.
[*The two women walk towards the exit.*]

SARAH: Wait till I get my hands on this carried-away oul' fool.

MARY-ANN: You couldn't houl' out to that, Sarah.

SARAH: Loves himself, he does. Tasty Sam. Him on the pension, too. I'll overcoat him when I get home. [*The two women exit.*]

BARNEY: How do you do it, man?

BUCKETS: That's it, Barney, the don't call me Buckets McGuinness for nothin'.

BARNEY: Come to think of it, why do the call you Buckets? That's a wild name.

BUCKETS: It was all to do with an Indian boat. [*Enter* LEG MCNAMARA] Ach, billy Leg, what about you? What are you havin'?

LEG: A bottle of stout.

BUCKETS: I'm just tellin' Barney here about why the call me Buckets.

LEG: Ah, that one. Well, you may tell it some other time. Barney, the lorry's just pulled up outside.

BARNEY: Heavens, I've forgot to leave the empties out the back. I'll do that nigh.

LEG: Do you wanna hand?

BARNEY: Not a'tall. I'll not be a minute. [BARNEY *exits.*]

BUCKETS: Take your time. [BUCKETS *walks in behind the bar, takes a long drink from a bottle of wine before filling a glass*] What are you havin', Leg?

LEG: Leave me out of it. If he catches you at that, you'll be a sorry man.

BUCKETS: If. [BUCKETS *comes out from behind the bar as* SWEENEY *enters.*]

SWEENEY: Is McKibben here?

LEG: Hasn't been in yet.

SWEENEY: Must be round in Benny's. [*He turns to exit.*]

LEG: Oh a Jimmy! Is the lad along with you the day?

SWEENEY: He is, aye. And he doesn't know his hook from his hand.

LEG: I know, I know. [*He is embarrassed.*] Will the get Sunday out of it?

SWEENEY: And Monday. [SWEENEY *exits.*]

LEG: Right, Jimmy. Thanks.

BUCKETS: Isn't it as well John Graham's not here. That'd be all we need. A shoutin' match to liven things up.

LEG: Aye, and this International Workers' Day.

BUCKETS: I forgot about that. The march is this mornin' then.

LEG: That's what I'm surprised at. I'd a thought it woulda passed this way b'nigh.

BUCKETS: Well, I haven't seen it. [BARNEY *enters.*] Barney, sure the parade hasn't passed this way yet?

BARNEY: Not that I've seen. It usually comes down Whitla Street and goes along Garmoyle Street, before finishin' across the street there.

BUCKETS: I'm sure there's one or two thirsty men walkin'.

LEG: I wonder what the turn-out was like.

BUCKETS: I'm sure they're not as big as they were in my day.

LEG: Ach, give over. You're like myself. You could count on the fingers of one hand the many times you marched.

BUCKETS: Sure, never mind. You don't have to be a priest to say prayers and we don't have to go marchin' to be workers. So, let's drink a toast to the workers, Leg. We mighten be able to march anymore, but we're still proud members of the Irish Transport & General Workers' Union.

LEG: Right.

BUCKETS: To the union!

LEG: To the union! [*They both stand and drink a toast. A brass band is heard.*] That sounds like it nigh.

BARNEY: That's it alright. [*The music gets nearer.*]

BUCKETS: I must have a wee luck. It's the least you can do. [*He walks over and holds open the front door, looking outside. He is joined by* LEG *and* BARNEY.] Oh, there's a brave crowd.

LEG: Can you see any of our fellas?

BUCKETS: I can't even see the union banner.

[HUGHIE MCNAMARA *appears and makes his way past the men into the bar. They all follow him inside as* BUCKETS *closes the door.*]

LEG: Oh, here's two-ton, fightin' Tony Galento. Are you not supposed to be at work?

HUGHIE: Don't worry, I'm only in for a quick bottle before I go back. Bottle of beer, Barney!

LEG: Is none of the committee comin' over?

HUGHIE: I'm sure they will. There's still speeches goin' on, so I nipped away a wee bit early since I've to go back to work.

BUCKETS: And McKibben and Henry turned up?

HUGHIE: Yep. Themens and John Graham paradin' side b'side. You'd think everything was just dead on.

LEG: Isn't it?

HUGHIE: How could it be?

LEG: But sure didn't I hear that Graham's suspension was lifted at the last meetin' and nigh you say they were friendly enough on the march. Everything must be alright.

HUGHIE: The only reason John's suspension was lifted was because he brought it to the attention of head office.

LEG: I'm sure Henry and McKibben weren't too happy about that.

HUGHIE: You better believe it. As I said, they're paradin' side b'side at the minute, but how long that'll last is anybody's guess.

BUCKETS: I've seen it all before.

HUGHIE: Don't worry. John's got plenty of backin' nigh.

LEG: Which reminds me. What's this I hear about you givin' lip to McKibben?

HUGHIE: So what?

LEG: So what! Who do you think you're talkin' to? Because I've a bad leg, don't think I wouldn't think twice about bringin' m'hand across your jaw!

HUGHIE: Okay, da, you win. Give it a rest till I finish my drink.

LEG: Just cut out the oul' cheek. And keep out of McKibben's road.

HUGHIE: Alright, alright, I'm sorry. Do you wanna bottle of stout?

[JOHN GRAHAM, JACK HENRY *and* MCKIBBEN *enter, rather noisily.*]

JOHN: And did you see the hack of oul' Banana Reilly tryin' to carry the union banner? Swayin' all over the place he was. [*They all laugh.*]

HENRY: No doubt he'd a few drinks before the parade, knowin' Banana.

MCKIBBEN: At least he turned up, not like some people. [*Looks at* BUCKETS]

BUCKETS: And listen to who's talkin', Karl McKibben Marx himself! Specially resurrected from the dead to lead the Belfast workin'-class to victory. I want the Finance Minister's job when you take over.

JOHN: And what qualifications have you?

BARNEY: Well, when he can outwit the likes of Sarah Montague over money, there must be some genius there.

[*The men laugh.* MCKIBBEN *calls a drink. More jokes are made as* HUGHIE MCNAMARA *takes* JOHN *to one side.*]

HUGHIE: Well, John, how is everything?

JOHN: Dead on, great.

HUGHIE: Are you sure?

JOHN: Of course.

HUGHIE: No problems?

JOHN: No.

HUGHIE: You don't want me to hang around?

JOHN: For God's sake, Hughie.

HUGHIE: Right then, I'll get back to work.

JOHN: Don't be workin' too hard.

HUGHIE: I bet you when I come by here at five a'clock, you'll be sittin' here drunk.

JOHN: No chance.

HUGHIE: See ya, then. See ya, da!

LEG: Right, Hughie son! [HUGHIE *exits.*]

BUCKETS: Who, Fargo A'Nail! I'll never forget the day he was caught walkin' out of the dock gates with a load of apples and oranges and even onions on him.

LEG: They sent for the peelers, didn't the?

BUCKETS: Aye, the Bulkies locked him in a room by himself until the cops came and the couldn't believe it when the couldn't find one single apple, orange or onion on him. He'd ate the lot! Skins and all!

LEG: And the had to let him go.

JOHN: Right, I'll tell you what. Since we're sort of celebratin the day, why don't you give us a song, Buckets?

HENRY: Aye, c'mon McGuinness, liven things up.

JOHN: We've all heard you singin' before. C'mon.

BUCKETS: I don't sing.

JOHN: Buckets. One song to start it off.

BUCKETS: Alright then, but only one.

LEG: That's the man.

MCKIBBEN: Away ya go.

[BUCKETS *steps forward and proceeds to sing* 'Days Gone By', *to the air of* 'I'll Tell Me Ma'.]

BUCKETS: 'Where I come from was right n'rough
We didn't always get enough
Times were hard but we got along
Stickin' together and singin' a song

Nobody shunned a tale of woe
People were friendly and nice to know
A neighbourhood steeped in joy and tears
Do you remember the bygone years.

Horses and carts and tramway lines
Annoyin' the peelers with finger signs
A jam-jar in to a picture show
Kissin' Mae West from the middle row.

Mitchin' school for dockside games
Sneakin' on ships till the sailors came
Bacon cuttin's and hairy pig's-feet
Kickin' futball in Nelson Street.

Do you remember those days gone by
A way of life we don't know nigh
People will tell you the times were bad
But they were the best bloody years I ever had.'

[*They all applaud, as* SARAH *and* MARY-ANN *enter from the street.*]

SARAH: Buckets McGuinness, could I have a word with you?

LEG: Oh-oh!

[SARAH *walks downstage and* BUCKETS *follows. She opens her purse and puts some money in his hand.* BUCKETS *is astounded, as* SARAH *and* MARY-ANN *exit to the snug.*]

BUCKETS: I don't believe this.

MCKIBBEN: What have you been doin' to deserve that?

JOHN: You must owe that wee woman a fortune b'nigh.

BARNEY: Yiz have got it all wrong. Sarah owed Buckets that money. N'that right, Buckets?

BUCKETS: No, Barney. I still owe her four pound eighteen shillins.

LEG: That's what I thought.

BARNEY: But what about the overcoat you sold her Sam?

BUCKETS: I never sold her Sam any overcoat. He bought it off a Dutch sailor in the bar.

BARNEY: Then why did you tell Sarah he bought it off you?

BUCKETS: To get rid of her.

BARNEY: oul' Sam musta been very drunk

BUCKETS: That's what's happened. That's it! [*He starts laughing.*] Oul' Tasty Sam's been that drunk he hasn't remembered who he bought the overcoat off. [*He slaps the money on the bar counter as they all cheer.*] Give everybody a drink, Barney! [*He holds up his glass.*] Here's to my good friend, Sarah Montague. Well, gentlemen, how'd the march go?

MCKIBBEN: It was a great march.

HENRY: Very good turn out.

JOHN: Not enough dockers, though.

MCKIBBEN: We'll get them out next year. Right?
[MCKIBBEN *holds out his hand to* JOHN. *They shake.*]

JOHN: Right.

MCKIBBEN: Listen. Let's drink a toast to the union.

BUCKETS: We've already done that.

MCKIBBEN: Well, we couldn't do it often enough. To the union!

ALL: To the union! [*They drink.*]

MCKIBBEN: And to International Workers' Day. [*They drink again.* JIMMY SWEENEY *and* DANNY-BOY *enter.*] Ah, there's Jimmy. C'mon to we have a drink, Jimmy.

DANNY-BOY: Hi, da.

LEG: Barney, give the lad whatever he wants there, will ye.

JOHN: Right, nigh that Buckets has done his piece, let's have Harry McKibben for a song! [*Cheers and applause*] Right, Harry, let's have ye.

MCKIBBEN: Okay, okay. I'll sing a rebel song. [*Cheers*]

HENRY: Go ahead, Harry.
[MCKIBBEN *proceeds to sing* 'Kevin Barry', *but after only a verse* SARAH MONTAGUE *and* MARY-ANN MCKEOWN *enter from the snug.*]

SARAH: What's all the singin' about, eh? Jasis, isn't it funny yiz only remember about the Republic with drink in yiz.

MCKIBBEN: Ah, give over, you weren't exactly decorated in the cause of Ulster.

SARAH: No, but I could sing about it a lot better than that.

JOHN: Right. C'mon, Sarah, you give us a song then.

LEG: That's a girl, Sarah.

BUCKETS: Give is ... 'Pennies From Heaven'. [*They all laugh.*]

SARAH: I was gonna sing 'The Sash', but I'll sing another good loyalist song instead.

MCKIBBEN: Okay, just this once. Let's hear it.

HENRY: Barney, you don't mind an Orange song on your premises?

BARNEY: Not a'tall.

JOHN: Right, a wee bit of order to we hear the woman singing. You're on the air, Sarah.

MARY-ANN: Do you want me to sing along with you, Sarah?

SARAH: In the name a Jasis, Mary-Ann McKeown, have some respect for yourself and your religion. Sit there and shut up!

MARY-ANN: Whatever you like nigh, Sarah, it's all the same to me.

[*They all laugh as* BUCKETS *joins in with* MARY-ANN *in saying her oft-repeated line, as above.* SARAH *proceeds to sing* 'The Green Grassy Slopes of the Boyne'. *In the middle of it,* BUCKETS *grabs her and dances round the bar with her, as does* JOHN. *The others laugh and cheer. They applaud as she finishes.*]

MCKIBBEN: Very good, Sarah, very good. You know we all have to live together in this city with our two religions.

HENRY: There's got to be toleration, respect for the other man's point of view.

MCKIBBEN: Yes, toleration is the key word.

JOHN: Definitely. Nigh that Sarah has sung, it's my pleasure to call upon the chairman of the union for a song. [*Applause*]

MCKIBBEN: Away you go, Jack.

MARY-ANN: Give is 'The Oul' Bog Road'.

HENRY: No thanks. I don't know any songs. All's I know is hymns. No, instead I'm sure the youngest man on the committee could give us a song or two. John Graham! [*Applause*]

MCKIBBEN: If he can sing as well as he can talk, he'll be alright.

LEG: Give is one of them latest ones.

HENRY: It's his own pleasure, nigh, his own pleasure.

JOHN: Well, I'd like to sing one song. And since this is International Workers' Day, I'd like to sing a workers' song.

BUCKETS: C'mon, John, ya boyo!

JOHN: This song was written by an Irishman, Jim Connell, one of the many Irishmen who've had to go abroad luckin' work.

MCKIBBEN: All because of England, mind you.

SARAH: You leave England out of this.

MCKIBBEN: Sure wasn't it England left Ireland the way it is. Men had to go away to get work.

SARAH: C'mon, Mary-Ann, if we're gonna be insulted over our religion, we'll get away out of this.

MARY-ANN: Whatever you like nigh, Sarah, it's all the same to me.

BUCKETS: Excuse me, Mrs. McKeown, but I understood you were of the Roman Catholic persuasion?

MARY-ANN: So a am.

BUCKETS: And you've been insulted?

MARY-ANN: Will you stop tryin' to complicate things. If Sarah wants to go, I'm goin' with her.

BUCKETS: If Sarah stuck her head in the fire, would you do it too?

MARY-ANN: No, I wouldn't.

SARAH: Are you comin' or what?

MARY-ANN: Whatever you like nigh, it's all the same to me.

[*All the men mimic* MARY-ANN *before the two women exit to the street.*]

MCKIBBEN: Right, back to the song. C'mon, John, I always liked an emigrant's song. You were sayin'?

JOHN: This one's not exactly an emigrant's song. This Irishman had obviously travelled a great deal and found that not only is the Irish workin'-class gettin' a raw deal, but so were the English workin' people and the French and the Germans and so on. So he wrote this song. [*He begins singing.*]
'The people's flag is deepest red
It's shrouded oft our martyred dead ...' [MCKIBBEN *stands bolt upright, Henry's face draws and* SWEENEY *puts down his drink.*]
'And ere their limbs grew stiff and cold
Their heart's blood dyed its every fold.'

MCKIBBEN: Hey! Cut that crap out, Graham! [JOHN *glances round at* MCKIBBEN, *but carries on singing.*]

JOHN: 'So raise the scarlet banner high
Beneath its folds ... '

MCKIBBEN: I said cut that crap out! [JOHN *stops singing.*] We don't want to listen to none of that Communist shit!

SWEENEY: And we're not goin' to.

HENRY: Change the song, Graham!

JOHN: But it's a workers' song. This is Workers' Day and we're union men.

MCKIBBEN: It's Commie shit!

JOHN: You can put whetever interpretation you want on it, but I feel like singin' it.

MCKIBBEN: Not round here you won't.

HENRY: Change the song, Graham.

JOHN: I thought you all believed in toleration. Remember? A while ago every man's view must be allowed for. Even your bigoted minds gave way to the singin' of a Protestant song. It's all very well to play at bein' trade union leaders, but when the true concept of Labour is raised, our leaders are terrified. Is that what's happenin' here? Is it not? My Labour song offends Labour leaders?

HENRY: You don't know the half of it! You have no idea what went into buildin' our union over the years.

JOHN: You built it?

HENRY: I put 25 years into it. How long have you put in?

JOHN: Twenty-five years of what?

HENRY: Twenty-five years of plenty and I'm fucked if I'm gonna stand round and let troublemakers like you wreck it.

JOHN: Who's wreckin'?

HENRY: You're wreckin'! How come nobody else is shoutin' their heads off? I don't know but I think one complainer out of a thousand men is a good record. A bloody good record!

JOHN: And why do they not complain', eh? Do you think the all enjoy shovin' and pushin' each other like animals in that pen every mornin'?

HENRY: What are you suggestin'?

JOHN: You know damn well what I'm suggestin'.

HENRY: You've made one remark too many, Graham.

JOHN: And what? You're gonna throw me off the committee? Don't worry, your days'll soon be over, Jack. The older dockers were easy meat, but there's younger men comin' after me and they won't accept the oul' ways.

HENRY: Don't have me laughing. [HENRY *chuckles.*]

MCKIBBEN: Why don't you take yourself off and spew that silly crap over somebody else?

SWEENEY: Aye, away and sing your 'Red Flag' round in the Labour Club. [BUCKETS *walks forward and takes* JOHN *by the arm.*]

BUCKETS: Aye, John, let it go this time. Let ignorant men have their way. [JOHN *shrugs him off.*]

JOHN: I've started it here and I'll finish it here. [*He resumes singing*]
'Look round the Frenchman loves its blaze
The sturdy German chants its praise ...'

MCKIBBEN: I warned you!

[*He lunges forward at* JOHN, *knocking him on to the floor.* LEG *takes* DANNY-BOY *to the side, away from the disturbance.* JOHN *carries on singing.* MCKIBBEN *pulls him back by the hair and kicks him repeatedly.* JOHN *folds up, but again starts singing.* HENRY *gives the nod and, this time, both* MCKIBBEN *and* SWEENEY *trail him outside, where a further beating takes place. Presently, the two men enter.*]

MCKIBBEN: He had that comin' to him.

HENRY: What? Take that from a gaunch like that? No sweat.

SWEENEY: Right, that's him sorted out. Let's have a drink. What are you havin', Leg?

LEG: What? Oh a ... a bottle of stout, Jimmy.

SWEENEY: Danny-boy?

DANNY-BOY: Glass a beer, thanks.

SWEENEY: Buckets?

BUCKETS: Nothin', nothin' for me.

[*Suddenly, the doors burst open and* THERESA GRAHAM *enters. She makes straight for* MCKIBBEN.]

THERESA: You bastard! [*She slaps him on the face.* MCKIBBEN *draws his fist back, but refrains.*] You no-good, cowardly, stinkin', bastard! You waited patiently on your chance, didn't ye, Harry McKibben!

MCKIBBEN: He asked for it.

THERESA: And I'm sure it didn't take much. The fact that he breathes a'tall is enough to annoy you.

MCKIBBEN: He's an agitator!

THERESA: And what does that make you?

MCKIBBEN: A better man than him.

THERESA: You wouldn't make a patch for John Graham's arse. He's a better man than you'll ever be.

MCKIBBEN: He's a communist.

THERESA: Well, God knows there must be something to recommend it, if ignorant men like you's against it.

HENRY: Would you not be better goin' on home?

THERESA: When I'm good and ready. And don't you stand there, Jack Henry, b'the way it's all nothin' to do with you. You've a lot to answer for. [*She glares around the pub.*] Yiz all have a lot to answer for. Whether yiz did the batin' or turned your backs, yiz are guilty, each and every one of yiz.

[LEG *takes her by the arm.*]

LEG: C'mon, Theresa girl, that's enough. [*She steps away from him.*]

THERESA: When I think of the times I told him he was wastin' his time. I told him the dockers weren't worth it, but he thought yiz were. There's a thin line between idealism and blindness, but it was no use talkin'.

MCKIBBEN: Go away and take him with you.

THERESA: Don't worry, we're goin', but don't be thinkin' yiz have seen the end of John Graham, for yiz haven't. He might as well see it through nigh. He'll be through them dock gates on Monday mornin', should I have to carry him myself.

MCKIBBEN: You just might have to carry him back through again.

THERESA: How can you be so full of badness, Harry McKibben? Why don't you leave us alone? First it was our Vera and nigh it's my husband. How far do you wanna go?

LEG: Let it go nigh, Theresa.

THERESA: Why doesn't he leave us alone? He's never satisfied unless he's hurtin' somebody. [*She points outside.*] He'll be back on Monday mornin'. I'll make sure of it. Should I have to carry him myself. [*She exits.*]

SWEENEY: That's women for ye. Here, Jack, yiz'll have to co-op a man on to the committee.

HENRY: Ah, that should be no problem. We can forget about him.

MCKIBBEN: C'mon, we'll sit down here outta the road.

HENRY: Aye, we could be doin' with a bit of peace and quiet.

SWEENEY: Send us in three bottles a stout, Barney. [*The three men exit to the snug. Offstage*] Did you know that Smith & Coggins are luckin' a new foreman this week?

MCKIBBEN: The must be gettin' a fair bit of work.

[*There is a prolonged silence in the bar.*]

BARNEY: Isn't that a terrible carry-on?

BUCKETS: Desperate. Give is it across the card, Barney. [BARNEY *proceeds to set up a bottle of stout and a whiskey.* BUCKETS *walks over to the end of the bar and takes down the union photograph from where it had been hanging on the wall. He throws it in the bin.*] That's another young man ruined b'the dock. And it wasn't drink done it this time. [*He knocks back his whiskey.*] I mustn't have enough drink in me. The barbed wire's cuttin' lumps outta me.

Black-out

WELCOME TO BLADONMORE ROAD

Welcome to Bladonmore Road was first performed at the Belfast Civic Arts Theatre, Belfast, May 1988. The set was designed by Houston Marshall. The director was Clive Brill. The cast was as followed:

Bernie McFadden	Stella McCusker
Alex McFadden	B.J. Hogg
Roisin Blakely	Linda Wray
Bill Blakely	Toby E. Byrne
Julia	Maureen Dow
Eamon Connery	John Guiney
Ignatius	Fabian Cartwright
Jan Blakely	Lynda Steadman

List of characters

Bernie McFadden, *age 50-plus.*
Alex McFadden, *age 41, Bernie's second husband, a self-made businessman.*
Ignatius, *age 21, Bernie's son, a gardener and part-time student.*
Julia, *age 66, Bernie's sister and lodger, fond of a drink.*
Roisin Blakely, *age 42, Bernie's new next-door neighbour, new-money posh.*
Bill Blakely, *age 48, Roisin's husband, a barrister, easy going.*
Jan Blakely, *age 20, the Blakely's adopted daughter, a student.*
Eamonn Conerney, *age 42, Bladonmore Road. Association Secretary and a Building Contractor.*

Welcome to Bladonmore Road is a comedy about a working-class family attempting to move up the social ladder by buying a house in the most exclusive neighbourhood of their city.

The play is set in the present in an exclusive street in one of the poshest areas of Belfast. With the minimum of changes it could be set in any city in the world.

ACT 1

SCENE 1

The new McFadden home. The living-room is in some disarray with various items of furniture and numerous boxes and bags scattered everywhere. A rhododendron bush, two-and-a-half feet high with large thick buds sits in a corner, its root ball in wrappings. Sam Cooke singing 'Twisting The Night Away' *is played over.* IGNATIUS, *aged 21, stumbles over something as he enters the room carrying a box. Music fades.*

BERNIE [*offstage*]: Watch m'bloody china!

IGNATIUS: It's alright, it's only oul' delph!

BERNIE: Oul' delph? That's Royal Bloody Albert! [*Puts box down*]

IGNATIUS [*mimics*]: Royal Bloody Albert.

　　[*He exits. Instantly, several items are thrown on-stage. These include a plastic mop bucket, a mop, brush, shovel, a couple of filled black plastic bags and lastly, a dartboard is rolled on.*]

IGNATIUS [*offstage*]: You're a bin lid, ma!

BERNIE: Shut up and keep goin'!

　　[BERNIE, *resplendent in a fur coat, is carried into room shoulder-high on an armchair by* IGNATIUS *and a removal man. They put the armchair down. The removal man exits.*]

IGNATIUS: Talk about a grand entrance.

BERNIE [*in affected posh accent*]: If we're going to live in style, we might as well enter in style.

IGNATIUS: Mammy, know who you look like sittin' there in that fur coat?

BERNIE [*normal accent*]: No, who?

IGNATIUS: Know your woman biz on TV. Vera ... Vera am ...

BERNIE: Vera Lynn?

IGNATIUS: No, Vera Duckworth.

BERNIE: Very funny. Where's the chile?

75

IGNATIUS: Bed.

BERNIE: Probably tired, God love her. Did she get her bottle?

IGNATIUS: Wouldn't take it.

BERNIE: Are y'sure you made her one?

IGNATIUS: 'Course a did.

BERNIE: Where's the Royal Albert?

IGNATIUS [*pointing*]**:** There.

   [*She goes over and starts taking the pieces out of the box.*]

BERNIE [*admiring each piece*]**:** Beautiful. [*Pause*] Y'know what you're gonna have t'do, Ignatius, don't ye?

IGNATIUS: What?

BERNIE: Go and see Nora Nugent and make arrangements for her t'come and breastfeed that chile every day.

IGNATIUS: What!

BERNIE: A chile that isn't breastfed takes til drink when it gets older, that's a well-known fact.

IGNATIUS: Don't talk spherical objects.

BERNIE: Ah know the two of yiz don't get on nigh, but ...

IGNATIUS: Don't get on! We hate each other! Well ... she hates me.

BERNIE: She doesn't hate ye.

IGNATIUS: Who? Four days after she had the baby, she handed it over to me on the steps of the maternity unit, and said that if she ever saw me or it again, she was immigratin' to Bangladesh.

BERNIE: God, four days. Most marriages take at least five years for the hatred to set in. Four days must be a record.

IGNATIUS: You're forgettin' something. I never married her.

BERNIE: Don't I know. Young fellas nighadays look on girls the way the DOE runs their car parks.

IGNATIUS: What are y'talkin' about?

BERNIE: 'Y'can come in, but I don't accept responsibility for loss or damage.'

IGNATIUS: Who has the baby then?

BERNIE: It's me that's rearing the poor wee thing.

IGNATIUS: I'm rearin' her.

BERNIE: Sure y'won't even change the chile's nappy?

IGNATIUS: A do. A just don't like the realllllll dirty ones. Anyway, Antoniette helps.

BERNIE: Not anymore.

IGNATIUS: Why not?

BERNIE: Your younger sister is refusin' to come and live up here.

IGNATIUS: Refusin'?

BERNIE: Says she's gonna live with her Granny McGlade.

IGNATIUS: Are you gonna let her?

BERNIE: She's 18, and God knows, when wee girls turn 18, their mothers turn into prison warders.

IGNATIUS: Ma?

BERNIE: What?

IGNATIUS: A think the neighbours have seen the coat.

[*As* BERNIE *takes off the coat, she sees the rhododendron bush.*]

BERNIE: What in the name of God's that?

IGNATIUS: What?

BERNIE [*pointing*]: That.

IGNATIUS: Oh, that's a bush a got for the garden.

BERNIE: Did you steal that outta work?

IGNATIUS: No

BERNIE: Y'sure?

IGNATIUS: Honest. Wee Bob the foreman let me take it.

BERNIE: But sure, this garden's already comin' down with lovely plants.

IGNATIUS: Aye, but no rhododendron. And any garden that hasn't got a rhody isn't a real garden. Besides, a got it for other reasons.

BERNIE: What other reasons?

IGNATIUS: It brings luck and good fortune,

BERNIE: Ignatius son, the longer you're in that job the more I worry about ye. Y'talk about plants and flowers as if they were people.

IGNATIUS: Ma, we originally came from plants.

BERNIE: From plants! Alex says it was monkeys and the catechism says it was Adam and Eve—y'wouldn't know who to believe. And what makes y'say this'll bring us money?

IGNATIUS: A didn't say money, a said, luck and good fortune.

BERNIE: Says who?

IGNATIUS: Wee Bob. He knows everything about plants and he says Rhododendrons come from China and over there, the people treat them like ... like a national treasure, they're so important Because of what they stand for.

BERNIE: And you believe that?

IGNATIUS: It's true. Y'see, it all goes back to a wee man called Chu Ling. Chu Ling lived—

BERNIE: Aye, well Chu Ling yourself and away out and plant it. And put it in a nice prominent part of the garden where I can see it.

IGNATIUS: Where's Camillus—he could be helpin' us?

BERNIE: I arranged for him to go round to our Evvie's after school and come up later. He'd only be in our way.

IGNATIUS: When's he startin' the new school?

BERNIE: Hopefully on Monday.

IGNATIUS: Ma, these schools up here won't stand for any trouble from our Camillus.

BERNIE: Camillus won't be any trouble.

IGNATIUS: What about the two classrooms he burned down?

BERNIE: That wasn't his fault. He told me, the sun magnified on to his matches and set them on fire.

[IGNATIUS *starts to unpack his record collection, made up entirely of Sam Cooke.*]

BERNIE: A thought you were sellin' them?

IGNATIUS: Sellin' m'music! Ma, a life without Sam Cooke would be like ... like, the countryside without grass.

BERNIE: Aye, and I know what sorta grass you're talkin' about.

IGNATIUS: Wise, ma.

[IGNATIUS *walks over to the glass-panelled double doors leading to the back garden and opens them.*]

IGNATIUS: Would y'luck at the state of that fuckin' garden?

BERNIE: Hey you!

IGNATIUS: What?

BERNIE: What did I tell you about usin' that language.

IGNATIUS: For godsake, ma.

BERNIE: Luck, I've already warned you. Bad language is one of the things that'll have to stop. This is the Bladonmore Road.

IGNATIUS: Aye, the snobbiest district in Belfast. I'll not be spendin' much time in it. I'll be goin' down every night to see my mates.

BERNIE: Most of your mates is on the bru.

IGNATIUS: I bet ye the play tennis and hockey up here. Pile a fruits. A tell ye what, there's plenty a space for the dogs in that garden.

BERNIE: I'm gettin' rid a them dogs. People up here don't keep mongrel dogs, Ignatius.

IGNATIUS: Mongrel! They're carefully crossed between an alsatian, a doberman pincher and Mick Curley's boxer. Specially designed to get the maximum amount of aggression.

BERNIE: I don't care if they're a cross between Lassie and Rin-Tin-Tin, they're not stayin' in this house.

IGNATIUS: Well, you can tell Camillus that.

BERNIE: Camillus can go and blurt! Nigh, c'mon til we get this house sorted out. We'll never get all this stuff put away before Alex gets home. By the way, where'd y'put his dartboard?

IGNATIUS: In the bin.

BERNIE: Don't have me cursin', Ignatius.

[IGNATIUS *shows her the dartboard. She breathes a sigh of relief and looks around the room.*]

BERNIE: It's hard t'believe, isn't it? Here we are—the McFaddens from dockland—nigh livin' on the Bladonmore Road. A've even got a new set of Royal Albert china. If my ma was alive nigh.

IGNATIUS: If your ma was alive nigh, that Royal Albert would go straight into some pawn.

BERNIE: Do you know, our house is the biggest on this side of the street?

IGNATIUS: Do y'not think, like, that Alex went a wee bit out of his depth?

BERNIE: Not a'tall.

IGNATIUS: He only owns a couple of takeaway chippies.

BERNIE: He's expandin'. He's gonna buy a restaurant. He doesn't know it yet, but ...

IGNATIUS: I still don't think he was mad about movin' up here.

BERNIE: He's all for it.

IGNATIUS: M'Aunt Julya says—

BERNIE: Your Aunt Julya nothin'. We're here and that's that.

IGNATIUS: It's all your top earners lives round here. I don't think Julya'll like it.

BERNIE: She can like it or lump it. She only lives with us, she doesn't rule us. Nigh, carry that out to the kitchen. [*The doorbell rings.*]

BERNIE: That'll be Alex.

IGNATIUS: I'll get it. [*He exits and returns with* ROISIN. ROISIN *is a well-dressed woman in her early forties.*] This is Mrs. Blakely from next door, ma.

ROISIN: How do you do? [*They shake hands.*]

BERNIE [*affected accent*]**:** Very well thank you. How are you doing yourself, Mrs. Blakely?

[IGNATIUS *stares at his mother upon hearing her accent.*]

ROISIN: Oh, call me Roisin. If we're going to be neighbours we might as well get on first name terms, don't you agree?

BERNIE: Oh yes, yes indeed, Roisin. I'm Bernadette and this is my son, Ignatius. [*He nods.*]

IGNATIUS: Call me Iggy.

BERNIE: I've a daughter called Antionette and another son, Camillus.

ROISIN: Oh, you've given your family beautiful names.

BERNIE: M'husband's name's Alex. But I wasn't responsible for that. [ROISIN *laughs politely.*]

ROISIN: Nooo. Well, I hope everything's going well and you're beginning to settle in?

IGNATIUS: We're only here an eyre.

BERNIE: Oh, everything's great and it's a very pitcheresk wee street.

ROISIN: We like it too. We've been here 12 years, that's me and my husband, Bill. He's chairman of our little Residents' Association. They do super work. Only last week he managed to get all residents to agree on the question of dogs defecating on the street.

BERNIE: Did he?

ROISIN: Oh my sister in London says it's a big issue over there too. So Bill has managed to get agreement that the owners are responsible. And when their dogs ... do it on the street, they must clean it up immediately.

BERNIE: That's a good idea, isn't it, Ignatius?

IGNATIUS: Oh definitely ma, you know how well-trained our dogs is.

ROISIN: Of course, they do expect you to join the Association.

BERNIE: Oh, put our names down.

ROISIN: It's really in all our interests.

IGNATIUS: Wait'll you meet our dogs.

BERNIE: Well, it was very nice of you to call in.

ROISIN: Not a'tall, my pleasure. I'm sure I'll meet your husband later on?

BERNIE: Oh, Alex is out running his business. He'll not be in til later on.

ROISIN: He's in business?

BERNIE: Restaurants.

ROISIN: Oh super. He must be all go.

BERNIE: Oh, somebody famous said once, that there's two types of people. Those who watch the world go round and those who make the world go round. Alex is the second type.

ROISIN: How interesting.

BERNIE: Oh, I fell on m'feet the day I met Alex McFadden.

IGNATIUS: Fell off your feet. Y'were out all day at a weddin' remember?

ROISIN: Well, I always think that moving house is very stressful. Did you have far to travel?

BERNIE: No, not really. North Belfast.

ROISIN: Oh, the Cavehill. My sister used to live on the Antrim Road. Beautiful, up there, isn't it? Did you live near the Cavehill?

BERNIE: Not ... too far away.

IGNATIUS: No. But for some strange reason, Gallahers factory horn used to shake the shite outiv our house in the mornins.

ROISIN: Well, the loudest thing you'll hear up here is the rustle of the trees in winter.

BERNIE: It does seem very quiet.

ROISIN: And I'm sure you'll get on famously with the neighbours. I'm on this side of you, but do you know who's on that side? I'll give you a clue. He's into ladies' underwear.

IGNATIUS: Does his wife know about it?

ROISIN: Ralph Johnston. You know—[*She sings and acts the catchline of a commercial*]—'Shop at Johnston's, The Quality Store'.

BERNIE: Oh yes, is that right?

ROISIN: Ralph is a super fella—a widower actually—you'll get on well with Ralph. And across from here is Doctor Walker, consultant surgeon at the Royal. He specialises on the brain.

IGNATIUS: Could my ma make an appointment?

ROISIN: Right, I really must be going. If there's anything you need, don't hesitate to ask.

BERNIE [*affected*]: Thank you, thank you very much.

ROISIN: Glad to have met you anyway.

BERNIE: And you too. Oh Roisin? [ROISIN *stops.*] My husband and I will be having a sort of ... celebration drink later on. Maybe you and your husband would like to join us?

ROISIN: Yes, yes, I'm sure Bill would love that.

BERNIE: About nine?

ROISIN: Smashing. Bye then.

BERNIE: See you later. [ROISIN *exits.*] She's a nice wonan.

IGNATIUS: Hey ma, where'd you get that accent?

BERNIE [*normal accent*]: What accent?

IGNATIUS: Y'sounded like you were tryin' t'speak and suck a pickled onion at the same time.

BERNIE: You mind your own business. A told yiz, everything's different nigh. If we're gonna live among these people, we can't go round talkin' as if we never went t'school.

IGNATIUS: But ma, you didn't go to school.

BERNIE: What's that got to do with it?

IGNATIUS: And where did Bernadette come from? Is Bernie out the windy nigh?

BERNIE: Ignatius, son?

IGNATIUS: What?

BERNIE: Shut your bake.

IGNATIUS: Here ma, you're not keepin' all these Mills & Boon books?

BERNIE: Up to my room.

IGNATIUS: Imagine! Mills & Boon at your age!

BERNIE: Ignatius son, if women were to give up on the notion of romance, there'd be no more use for men. Women don't marry men for what the are, the marry them for what the hope the can change them into. That's what romance is.

IGNATIUS: Where does Alex fit into all this?

BERNIE: He doesn't—he's m'husband.

IGNATIUS: M'Aunt Julya says there's only one way to treat men.

BERNIE: How's that?

IGNATIUS: With contempt.

BERNIE: She'd know, and her couldn't get a man.

IGNATIUS: She says there was one man she nearly married when she was 21.

BERNIE: Aye, Charlie Harvey. He tuck her out one night and bought her drink all night. At 12 a'clock Charlie says t'her, 'Hy're y'feelin' nigh?' She says, 'Oh A'm warmin' up nigh.' He says, 'Y'should. You've the price a two begs a coal in ye.' He saw then she tuck too much drink.

IGNATIUS: She never told me that one.

BERNIE: Aye, well, I should know, she's my sister.

[*Low sound of dogs barking*]

IGNATIUS: Shhhh! Do you hear something?

BERNIE: Where?

IGNATIUS: Out the back.

[*He goes to back doors. Loud sound of dogs barking.* JULIA*enters out of breath. Aged 66. She is holding two dog leads, and a handbag and looks dishevelled and distressed.*]

BERNIE: In the name a God.

IGNATIUS: Aunt Julya, y'look as if you've just been dragged through a hedge.

JULIA [*attempting to shout*]: A was dragged throush a hedge! [*She waves the dog leads.*] Them bloody dogs. [*She lifts up her dress.*]

JULIA: Caught m'good drawers on a wire fence, a did—Ralph came and helped me down,

BERNIE: Ralph?

IGNATIUS: The man next door.

BERNIE: A know he's the man next door.

JULIA: Very nice man. Lovely head a hair.

BERNIE: Christ, what is my new neighbours gonna say? Roisin'll think we're not gonna use the front door. And I told you I wasn't bringin' them dogs up here.

JULIA: Sure what coulda do? Young Camillus loves them so he does. But, by frig, if I hadda had a gun the day, I'da shot them m'self.

IGNATIUS: How did you get up here?

JULIA: Two bloody buses. On the first bus the conductor would only let me take them upstairs—acourse it's more like them takin' me—the two big brutes, God forgive me. Well, as soon as I sat down upstairs, didn't Brandy get up and shite all over the bus. [BERNIE *tut-tuts in disgust.*] I was mortified. A got off at the next stop without a word to a sinner. God, I'm chokin'.

IGNATIUS: And then what happened?

JULIA: On the second bus, Bruce tuck a likin' for the woman's messages that was sittin' fernenst me. Before I know it, there was spuds and callyflyer all over the bus.

IGNATIUS: What did the woman say?

JULIA: She didn't say nothin' t'me. For I sat with m'face stuck up against the windy. The coulda been eatin' the poor woman's leg, but was I gonna let on? Bernie, it was terrible. I was distracted, distracted a was, fit t'be tied.

IGNATIUS: How did you get off the bus?

JULIA: Waita y'hear. The woman called the conductor. And when he came up t'put the dogs off, where did the two cowardly pigs go? Under my feet! I had d'let on a was afraid a them. But acourse, as soon as I got up t'go, who followed me down the stairs—like greyhounds outiv a trap? Frig, if I hadda had a gun! A dropped m'pension book and everything, a did.

BERNIE: It serves y'right.

IGNATIUS: No, I think y'did a great job, Julya. Y'deserve a medal.

JULIA: Could a have a wee drink instead?

BERNIE: Make her a cup a tea. And Ignatius, see where them dogs are. [IGNATIUS *exits.*]

JULIA: Oh Bernie, did y'hear about Sally Anne Joss?

BERNIE: No, what?

JULIA: Roomatroid ardritis.

BERNIE: Ach, away.

JULIA: Riddled with it, she is. Says she to the doctor, 'Doctor, does this mean a have t'cut back on sex?' Says he, 'Oh, once every couple a months would be plenty.' Says she, 'Doctor, if I was able t'get him interested once every couple a months, a wouldn't care if a'd terminal cancer.' [*They laugh.*] She's a terrible case, Sally Anne.

BERNIE: Sure, d'ya mind the time her man drunk his wages and got on the Liverpool boat stocious drunk?

JULIA: Will y'ever forget it?

BERNIE: He sent Sally Ann a wire the next day luckin' his fare back

to Belfast. She sent him a note sayin', 'We're alright here, if
you're alright there.' [*The two women laugh.*]

JULIA: B'God, in them days the men got away with murder too,
didn't the?

BERNIE: We'd some quare times in thon oul' district.

JULIA: I often wonder if we had it to do all over again, would we a
done it any different?

BERNIE: Maybe you shoulda got married.

JULIA: And where woulda a got a man?

BERNIE: Y'had your chances.

JULIA: Chances m'arse.

BERNIE: And it wasn't for the want a luckin'.

JULIA: Guilty. Yes, I'm guilty of that. [*Proclaims*] I'm a woman in search
of a man! And a've been searchin' for 66 years. The only man I
ever loved was m'da. In 66 years, a've yet d'meet a decent man.

BERNIE: No decent man would put up with your drinkin'.

JULIA: Don't talk to me about decent men. Jimbo McGlade didn't
exactly treat you like a Greek Goddess.

BERNIE: You know Julya, he's dead fourteen years and I still have
nightmares of him comin' to bate me.

JULIA: Well, y'landed on your feet with Alex McFadden, let me tell
you, Bernie McGlade. And if the last two years is anything to go
by, you'll be lucked after til y'go to your grave.

BERNIE: A know, Alex is a good fella.

JULIA: I don't know how y'did it. Him a Protestant, and ten years
younger than ye!

BERNIE: Alex likes my ... maturity.

JULIA: And you like his money.

BERNIE: Well a married for romance the first time, a thought I'd try
it for money this time. [IGNATIUS *enters with tray of cups etc.*]

IGNATIUS: Tea up, ladies.

JULIA: Thanks, Ignatius son.

IGNATIUS: I'm away to find these dogs. [*He exits.*]

JULIA: I mind the first time I saw you on his arm Bernie, a thought a
was gonna have kittens. He lucked so ... so innocent beside you.

BERNIE: Whadaya mean?

JULIA: A mean, he lucked so young and ... and handsome beside
you. [BERNIE *glares at* JULIA.] Ach will, y'know what a mean. Nigh
I mind the time when you lucked like your woman
whadayacaller ... Claudette Colbert—[BERNIE *touches up her hair
at the memory*]

BERNIE: Alex says I luck sexy even when a'm countin' up m'debts.

JULIA: Ignatius says I luck like a corpse when a'm countin' up m'debts. It's terrible what time does to your face, isn't it? What it has tuck thousands of years to do to the Glens of Antrim, time has done to my face in 66 years. Sometimes when a luck in the mirror a feel like the Cliffs a Dineen. That's why I hate anybody singin' that song, I think a my face.

BERNIE: I don't think I've done too bad.

JULIA: Bernie dear, where I have a few wee tributaries you've some of the biggest rivers in Ireland.

BERNIE: Alex doesn't think so. He says the lines on my face are rose-scented pathways to my heart.

JULIA: Oh excuse me.

BERNIE: And when he bought this house he said it was to be our 'Shalimar'.

JULIA: Shaliwhat?

BERNIE: Julya, Alex McFadden is a self-made, educated man. He knows how to use words.

JULIA: Who? He's a wee, jumped-up, schemin' Prod from the backstreets of Belfast.

BERNIE: Well, you'll be glad to live under his roof.

JULIA: Nigh, I don't know about that. It's a lovely house and all that but I don't know if I'll stick it up here.

BERNIE: Julya love. Get one wee thing into your head afore we go any further. This is for keeps. Sure y'could never have dreamed of us livin' on the Bladonmore Road. This is literally the house of my dreams.

JULIA: It's not the house I'm talkin' about, Bernie.

BERNIE: What is it then?

JULIA: The people.

BERNIE: Sure, it's all professional people lives round here.

JULIA: That's what a mean.

BERNIE: What do y'mean?

JULIA: They've money, they're different from us.

BERNIE: But sure we're not doin' too badly ourselves.

JULIA: But they've always had money.

BERNIE: Julya, your head's full a Carlsberg Specials.

JULIA: A know, a need a drink, have yiz found out where the nearest pub is?

BERNIE: Why do you always have to have a drink?

JULIA: Confidence. A wee drink gives me confidence. Other people are born with it, I have d'buy it. That's what I say to Mickey Kelly in the Rocktown. 'Mickey buy is a wee bottle a confidence and a'll give ye a kiss.'

BERNIE: There is no pubs round here.

JULIA: No pubs! But sure a district with no pubs would be like the post office without my pension money.

BERNIE: Julya, this isn't down our way. People round here have more to do with their time than sit in pubs.

JULIA: A know. Havin' t'make money is a terrible infliction. What about a club, if there's no pubs, there must be a wee club tucked away somewhere?

BERNIE: There is clubs. But not the sort you're thinkin' of. We're puttin' our name down for the Golf Club.

JULIA: Golf Club! Does that mean y'have t'play a game a golf afore y'get a drink?

BERNIE: It's a very exclusive membership.

JULIA: Well, a suppose if the sell drink, y'may put my name down for membership too.

BERNIE: A doubt if your pension would stretch that far.

JULIA: Why?

BERNIE: It's £300 to join and £250 a year after that.

JULIA: Oh, Holy Hell's Bells and Blazes! The wee Engineers' Club is only eight quid—and that's for a married couple.

BERNIE: A told ye it was exclusive.

JULIA: Exclusive! A wouldn't pay that money t'get into Heaven. Give me the Saturday night singsong down in the wee Rocktown Bar anytime.

BERNIE: That just suits ye.

JULIA: Do the even have a singsong in this millionaire's club? Not a'tall. I heared that people with money don't sing. When the go out the wouldn't let themselves down b'singin'. They just sit around and drink. The men talkin' about the price a houses and cars and the women plannin' when they're next gettin' their legs waxed.

[JULIA *stands up and finishes her tea. She moves to the back doors, fixing her hair and straightening her clothes.*]

BERNIE: Well, I've met the woman from the next house and she's very nice. A very attractive lookin' woman.

JULIA: And that's another thing! I heared there's wife-swappin' goes on in these fancy areas! [JULIA *moves to exit*]

BERNIE: Where are you goin'?

JULIA: In d'see Ralph.

BERNIE: What?

JULIA: The search goes on, Bernie—even on the Bladonmore Road!
[*She exits.* BERNIE *rushes after her.*]

BERNIE: Come back here. Y'carried away fool ye, come back d'hell a that!

SCENE 2

IGNATIUS *enters downstage right, in or about the back garden area. He looks about and then whistles with his fingers in his mouth. Then he shouts with his hand cupped around his mouth.*

IGNATIUS: Brannnnnnnnnnnnnnnndy! Bruuuuuuuuuuuuuuuuce!
[*He looks up and down. Just at this a girl, aged 20, enters downstage right and walks past him. She is carrying some files and books. She ignores him. He stares after her. When she exits he runs after her, shouting the dogs names and whistling.*]

SCENE 3

The Blakely home. In a workroom with several picture frames, canvases, paint pots etc. lying about. BILL BLAKELY *is standing at an easel painting. His jersey, trousers and shoes have a smattering of paint marks.* ROISIN *enters.*

ROISIN: Oh Bill—[*exasperated*]—the car's broken down again.

BILL [*concentrating on his painting*]**:** Good heavens, what a surprise.

ROISIN: It's alright for you—I'm fed up.

BILL: What is it this time? Driving without oil again?

ROISIN: Do you know how long I waited on the garage coming out? An hour and ten minutes. And trust me to break down beside a building site. This young fella actually came over to me and do you know what he said?

BILL: 'Aren't you Bill Blakely's wife, the spendthrift?'

ROISIN: Funny. He asked me was I wearing a bra? I mean, the barefaced cheek of it.

BILL: What did you say?

ROISIN: I gave him my phone number. [*Pause*] I said I gave him my phone number.

BILL [*ignoring her*]**:** Good for you.

ROISIN: You approve?

BILL: Wholeheartedly.

ROISIN: You wait, Bill Blakely, 'til I run off with a big, muscle-bound hod-carrier.

BILL: Just make sure to leave all your plastic cards before you go.
[*She recognises the painting.*]

ROISIN: Hey, that's the Bridge at Cushendun.

BILL: So.

ROISIN: You said you were doing Gweedore.

BILL: Changed my mind.

ROISIN: See you! [*She mockingly chokes him.*]

ROISIN: Bill, seriously, I need a new car. [*He laughs.*] I do. That's four times in four weeks, I've been left stranded. Only saw my father once last month.

BILL: You've heard of walking.

ROISIN: You don't walk too far.

BILL: I work.

ROISIN: I'll be back to work soon enough.

BILL: Good. Then you'll have the money to buy a car.
[*She pushes his arm as he is about to paint and walks away. He immediately puts down his brush and chases after her. He grabs her from behind and they playfully wrestle.* JAN *enters.*]

ROISIN [*trying to escape*]**:** Don't you dare.

JAN: Ahem. [*They part.*] Eamonn Conerney just rang. He's on his way over.

ROISIN: Yes, dear.

JAN: I'm going down to the students' union for a while.

ROISIN: Okay, dear. [JAN *turns to go.*] I mean, no dear. Jan we've been invited in to meet the family next door and I'd like you to come too.

JAN: Ach, mum.

ROISIN: It'll only be for ten minutes.

JAN: But I've arranged to meet people.
[BILL *returns to his easel.*]

BILL: It won't take that long, Jan. [*She tuts and turns to go.*]

ROISIN: Jan. [*She turns back.*] Your father and I want to talk to you about something else. This Bahai religion—

JAN: What about it?

ROISIN: You tell us.

JAN: There's nothing to tell.

ROISIN: What in God's heaven's name has gotten into you?

BILL: Perhaps you'd like to talk it over with us?

JAN: I'm over eighteen, I can practise whatever religion I like.
[*JAN turns to go.*]

ROISIN [*shouting after her*]**:** And it's time you put on some decent clothes.
[*JAN exits. EAMONN enters. He is a slight man, wearing a three-piece suit and thin, gold-rimmed glasses.*]

EAMONN: Family tensions?

BILL: What would life be without them?

EAMONN: I just called by. Can't make the Bridge tonight, chaps.

BILL: Not allowed, Eamonn?

EAMONN: I can't, Bill. Can't get out of this meeting.

BILL: What meeting?

EAMONN: The Chapel. Father White—

ROISIN: The new priest. I told you about him, Bill.

EAMONN: He's a bit of a shite really. Insisting on dominating every committee, every meeting.

ROISIN: Everything was fine before he arrived.

BILL: Oh, the modern Catholic Church. So insecure. Will you be at the club tomorrow night?

EAMONN: Oh, yes, definitely. What about our new neighbours— have they moved in yet?

BILL: Yes, yes actually they have. Roisin has met them.

ROISIN: I think you'll find them very ... interesting.

EAMONN: Well, make sure they receive the Committee literature.

BILL: As you wish, Mr. Secretary. In fact, we've been invited in for a drink.

EAMONN: That's a good start.

BILL: Let's hope so.

EAMONN: Right, I better go. Oh and Bill, don't forget to let us know as soon as they make an offer on Lynda's claim.

BILL: Your wife's claim. That's all I hear. 'Your-wife-tripping-over-a-soldier-lying-in-a-garden-in-Turf-Lodge'. Are you sure Lynda wasn't lying in the garden with him.

EAMONN: At least my wife visits her clients. You wouldn't be seen dead in Turf Lodge. [*The phone rings.*]

BILL: Go to the top of the class, Conerney. [*Exits. ROISIN advances amorously towards EAMONN. EAMONN backs away.*]

EAMONN [*quietly*]**:** You weren't in when I phoned this morning.

ROISIN [*quietly*]**:** Aerobics.

[*As* ROISIN *advances,* EAMONN *backs up against Bill's easel, knocking it to the floor. He panics, re-standing the easel while she laughs.*]

EAMONN: So what about tomorrow?

ROISIN: Should be alright. I'll ring you.

[BILL *re-enters*]

BILL: That was Ralph.

EAMONN: Ralph?

BILL: He sounds very agitated. Wants us down straight away.

EAMONN: What's wrong with him?

ROISIN: What did he say?

BILL: Something about a crazed woman banging at his back door.

SCENE 4

IGNATIUS *is sitting rocking and hushing his baby to sleep.* BERNIE *comes storming in fron the kitchen. The room is now in some sort of order. At downstage left, the rhododendron is freshly planted.*

BERNIE: Camillus! [*To* IGNATIUS] Where's that Camillus one? He's only here ten minutes and he's ate them two corned Squares I was keepin' for m'tea. [*Shouting off*] Camillus!

IGNATIUS: Mammy, shush!

BERNIE [*tenderly*]: Give is her and I'll put her down. M'wee pet.

[BERNIE *takes the baby and puts her in a carry-cot nearby.*]

IGNATIUS: A think she's away, anyway.

BERNIE [*to baby*]: Ach m'wee darlin. God love her, luck at her. Isn't she just beautiful, my wee Lorenzia.

IGNATIUS [*angry*]: Ma!

BERNIE: What?

IGNATIUS: You know what! Her name is Julie and that's what I want her called, Julie! Okay?

BERNIE: Julie! Sure that's as plain as a plate a champ.

IGNATIUS: I like it. And I'm her father.

BERNIE: I prefer Lorenzia. It's on the birth certificate as her second name, remember?

IGNATIUS: You threatened me.

BERNIE: I threatened you?

IGNATIUS: You said if I didn't give her Lorenzia you wouldn't look after her. All because of some obscure Italian saint.

BERNIE: I know! Why not call her both?

IGNATIUS: What?

BERNIE: Julie Lorenzia.

IGNATIUS: Aye, and we could paint her arse red and white stripes.

BERNIE: Ignatius, shut your trap.

[BERNIE *searches for her make-up bag and starts to paint her face at a mirror.*]

BERNIE: Where's your Aunt Julya?

IGNATIUS: Lyin' down for a while. Then—surprise, surprise—she's goin' down to the Rocktown when she gets up.

BERNIE: God, there's nearly nine a'clock. Them people next door's gonna be here any minute and no sign of Alex McFadden.

IGNATIUS: Alex is an entrepreneur. Probably workin' late cookin' the books.

BERNIE: Alex doesn't do that.

IGNATIUS: Ma, since the Industrial Revolution, there hasn't been a businessman yet who didn't cook the books.

BERNIE: That reminds ne.

IGNATIUS: What does?

BERNIE: This is my night-class night. I forgot all about it.

IGNATIUS: Y'could hardly go tonight. I'll not be goin' t'mine this week.

BERNIE: We were t'do poetry tonight.

IGNATIUS: And how are y'managin' with the old squawkin' talkin'?

BERNIE: I don't like it.

IGNATIUS: Good start.

BERNIE: I told him. The teacher asked me which of the poets we were readin' did I like, and I told him, a didn't like none of them.

IGNATIUS: Why not?

BERNIE: Because a couldn't understand them that's why. So I said thin, 'What's the good of somebody writin' a poem that has t'be explained t'people?'

IGNATIUS: And what did he say?

BERNIE: He said it keeps him in a job.

BERNIE 'Oh that's it,' says I. 'The people that writes weird poems does it to keep schoolteachers in jobs.' I told him I could write better m'self.

IGNATIUS: And what'd he say?

BERNIE [*meekly*]: I've to have three poems in for next week.

IGNATIUS And have y'written them?

BERNIE: Ignatius son, I haven't got a friggin' clue. A started writin' one last week about the pleasures of bringin' up children.

IGNATIUS: And?

BERNIE: B'the time a got near the end, a wanted t'go downstairs and bate Camillus black and blue. [*We hear dogs barking loudly.*]

IGNATIUS: That'll be Camillus nigh.

BERNIE: Where was he?

IGNATIUS: Takin' the dogs for a walk round the new district.

BERNIE: Go and get him, Ignatius! And tell him them dogs is not to leave that garden. [IGNATIUS *exits through the front door.* BERNIE *follows him to the front door. She shouts off*] And tell him when I get him, he's gettin' a good kick in the ... [*She suddenly remembers the neighbours. Affected*] ... Tell him he's been a bold boy! [*At this Bernie's husband,* ALEX MCFADDEN, *arrives, carrying boxes of frozen hamburgers.*]

ALEX: What's goin' on?

[*He stops, kisses her on the cheek, before entering to unload.*]

BERNIE: Camillus is runnin' the streets with them dogs.

ALEX: Sure that's alright, the dogs need exercise.

BERNIE: Exercise! The woman next door doesn't allow shitin' in the street.

ALEX: What?

BERNIE: Ach, nothin'. Where y'goin' with all them hamburgers.

ALEX: The fridge is broke down in the shop. S'only for a few days. Is there anything wrong, love?

BERNIE: Oh no, not a'tall. But do you have to parade in and out in front of the neighbours on our first day here with boxes of frozen hamburgers?

ALEX: A have to get them in the fridge Bernie or they'll go off and I'd lose cabbage.

BERNIE: What'll the neighbours think? I told Roisin you were in the restaurant business. She'll probably think we're gonna sell hamburgers out the front door nigh.

ALEX: That reminds me. The purchase of the new shop has been completed and we'll be in full operation within a month or two.

BERNIE: Which one's this nigh?

ALEX: The one near here. The one that used to be a doctor's surgery or something. Bernie, you don't take the slightest interest in my business deals.

BERNIE: A do, a do. It's just that I'm more interested in the 'book-keeping' side of things.

ALEX: This shop is ideally situated upon the main road. There isn't another Hot Food Bar within a two mile radius of Bladonmore Road. It'll be a wee goldmine.

BERNIE: What will you be sellin'?

ALEX: The usual stuff.

BERNIE: Alex pet, maybe these people up here might want something more than fish and chips and hamburgers.

ALEX: Don't you worry, I've all that sussed out, for a start, with their hamburgers, the'll be able to order sauces, mushroom sauces and pepper sauces, and coleslaw and them sort of things. But I know that well-heeled people wants even more than that, so, I'm gettin' prawns and squid and all the other rare fish stuff. Big Trevor's doin' a deal with an Ardglass fisherman.

BERNIE: Here, all that stuff's very expensive.

ALEX: Bernie love, expensive gear for expensive tastes. I know m'markets. Nigh, can a get the rest of these in? [*Meaning to exit*]

BERNIE: Alex?

ALEX: What?

BERNIE: Give us a kiss?

ALEX: Whattt! [*She goes over to him.*]

BERNIE: A just want t'say thank you. [*They embrace.*]

ALEX: Thank you, for what?

BERNIE: Where would I be without you?

ALEX: Probably walkin' the streets at the Albert Clock.

BERNIE: But you did all this for me. A just wish m'ma was still livin' to see all this.

ALEX: Don't tell me a'd have your ma as well as Julya!

BERNIE: A've finally come up in the world, thanks t'you.

ALEX: Good, nigh a have t'get the rest of these burgers in.

BERNIE: No, but listen, tell me. Do y'think you'll like it up here?

ALEX: Why shouldn't a?

BERNIE: Are y'happy?

ALEX: A was happy enough where we were, but ... what's the odds. As long as you're happy, I'll motor on.

[*They kiss.* IGNATIUS *enters.*]

IGNATIUS: Jesus Christ. Spencer Tracey and Katharine Hepburn. I got the dogs tied up.

BERNIE: Where's Camillus.

IGNATIUS: He's away over t'play with some wee lad who has a rabbit.

BERNIE: Well, I'm away up t'change.

ALEX: T'change?

[BERNIE *picks up the baby.*]

BERNIE: Roisin and Bill will be here any minute. [*To baby*] There's my wee Julie Lorenzia. Sleepin' away—shh, nigh. [*She exits.*]

ALEX: Who the fuck's Roisin and Bill?

IGNATIUS: M'ma has invited the next door neighbours in for a drink.

ALEX: That was quick.

IGNATIUS: Well, y'know Bernie. She does everything quick. She was only married six months when she had me.

ALEX: Cut that out. Here, carry them hamburgers into the kitchen, and give me a hand in with the rest.

IGNATIUS: Hamburgers! Suppose these are hot!

ALEX: How can they be hot when they're frozen?

IGNATIUS: Y'know what a mean. [*Winking*] Aren't you a capitalist?

ALEX: Let me tell you smart-arse. I do an honest day's work.

IGNATIUS: How can ye? Sure y'make a profit.

ALEX: It's better that what you're doin'. Flower arrangin'. And readin' books. The only thing anybody got from readin' books was bad eyesight. I could put you on the road in a kebab van.

IGNATIUS: Put me on the road? That would put me round the bend.

ALEX: Kebabs is all the rage nigh.

IGNATIUS: So is condoms. But I'm not gonna start sellin' them! Business is for crafty people, Alex. Intelligent people look for something more honest.

ALEX: I know what's gonna happen t'you with all this education. You're gonna end up in a dead-end job like ... like teachin' or the civil service or worse. Y'could end up a ... a ... a solicitor—everybody knows, all solicitors is crooks. Even their mistresses don't like solicitors. Or it could be even worse! You could end up an estate agent. Or a doctor or a dentist. Do you know some dentists drill holes in peoples' teeth, then tell them there's holes in their teeth and that the need a gold fillin'? And you talk to me about capitalism? I'm tellin' ye, Ignatius kid, education can corrupt even the most well-intentioned mind.

IGNATIUS: It won't corrupt me.

ALEX: Aye, you'd shite coalbrick if you'd a square-arsed hole. [*The doorbell rings.* ALEX *goes to answer.*] Ignatius, son, remember, see every corner you ever turn, I probably sold hamburgers at it.

[*He opens the door.* BILL *and* ROISIN BLAKELY *enter dressed in identical his and hers track suits.*]

BILL: You must be Mr. McFadden. I'm Bill Blakely, chairman of the street Residents' Association, and this is my wife, Roisin. And my daughter, Jan. [*They shake hands.*]

ALEX: How do yiz do? Pleased to meet y'love.

ROISIN: Hello. I met your wife, Bernadette.

ALEX: Aye, she was sayin'. This here's Iggy.

ROISIN: Yes, we've already met.

IGNATIUS: I'll just get the rest of these ...

[*He exits to the kitchen with the hamburgers.*]

ALEX: Sorry about the mess of the place.

ROISIN: Where is the lady of the house anyway?

ALEX: Nipped upstairs for a minute.

[*At this* BERNIE *enters, made up, expensive full-length, backless dress, high-heels etc.*]

ROISIN: Speak of the devil. Bernadette, I want you to meet my husband, Bill. And my daughter, Jan. She's at university. [*They shake hands.*]

BERNIE: Very pleased to meet yiz all.

BILL: Very pleased to meet you, Mrs. McFadden.

BERNIE [*affected*]: And you too, Mister Blakely.

BILL: I hope you like your new house?

BERNIE: Absolutely super it is, super.

BILL [*to* ALEX]: Oh, by the way, is that your van outside?

ALEX: It is, aye.

BILL: I think I saw two, possibly three, large dogs inside it, having one hell of a good time.

ALEX [*rushing out*]: Fuck—m'hamburgers!

BILL: Oh.

BERNIE: It's alright, he was just after informing me he brought the children home a couple of hamburgers for a snack.

[IGNATIUS *enters and exits through front door.*]

BERNIE: Like we're all upside down at the moment with the moving and that, that's why the children are having hamburgers, they usually have squid and prawns on a Friday night.

[ALEX *enters with two empty boxes, one in each hand.*]

ALEX: Dirty fuckin' bastards!

BERNIE: Alex!

ALEX: Oh sorry. My goodness, our pet dogs have just cost me a packet.

[IGNATIUS *enters and exits to kitchen with more hamburgers.*]

IGNATIUS: That's the lot.

BERNIE [*clearing her throat*]: Alex, I think perhaps our guests would like a drink.

ALEX: Right. [*He scours about the room until he finds a large cardboard box.*] Nigh, the selection isn't great, we haven't sorted ourselves out yet. What do you fancy, Roisin?

ROISIN: Gin and tonic would be fine, Alex.

[*Searches. Pulls up a bottle of sherry*]

ALEX: That's sherry. [*And again*] Another sherry. [*And again*] Another sherry.

ROISIN: Who drinks all the sherry?

ALEX: Bernie's sister, Julya, you haven't met her yet. Sorry Roisin, no gin.

ROISIN: I suppose I'll have a sherry then.

ALEX: No problem. One sherry comin' up. Yourself Bill?

BILL [*apprehensively*]: Whiskey? [ROISIN *gets her drink.*]

ALEX [*confidently*]: Should be a whiskey. No whiskey. Fancy a sherry, Bill?

BILL: I'll try a sherry.

ALEX: Jan?

JAN: Orange juice please.

ALEX: That we do have. One orange juice comin' up.

[IGNATIUS *enters just in time to snap the orange juice from Alex's hand and present it to* JAN. *They smile at each other.*]

ALEX: And what about you, love?

BERNIE: Cointreau with ice, dear.

ALEX Do you want a slice of lemon in it or do you prefer cherries?

BERNIE [*smiling*]: Alex likes to be clever.

ALEX: One sherry Cointreau comin' up. [*Pours* BERNIE *a drink*] Ah'll get the drinks cabinet sorted out the marra, Bernie love.

BILL: Well. Cheers. And welcome to Bladonmore Road.

REST: Cheers. [*They all drink.*]

BILL: I understand you're in the restaurant business, Mr. McFadden?

ALEX: Ach, yeah shift a bit a grub here and there.

BILL: Sounds good.

ALEX: Whadaya do yourself?

BILL: Law, I'm afraid.

ALEX: Law?

ROISIN: Bill's a solicitor.

ALEX: That's a ... that's a good job.

BERNIE That's what I want my Camillus t'be.

ALEX: There's a fortune to be made at that game. With legal aid and all that. When you've won a claim for somebody, you tell them the money hasn't come through yet, but you keep it in your bank account, coppin' the interest right?

BILL: I have heard of that being practised.

BERNIE: Mr. Blakely, do you ever do any of the big court cases that biz on TV.

BILL: One or two.

ROISIN: He's being modest. Bill Blakely is one of the most successful solicitors in Northern Ireland.

BILL: Roisin.

ROISIN: Bill's name is never out of the papers.

BERNIE: Alex's name was in the paper last week, wasn't it Alex?

ROISIN: What for, Alex?

ALEX: Ach, it was nothin'.

BERNIE: Tell them Alex.

ALEX: Ach, it was just the oul' darts.

BERNIE: He finished on a ten-darter in the finals.

BILL: Well done, Alex. I play the odd game of darts myself.

ALEX: I like it. All the mates throw too.

BERNIE: And I'm taking driving lessons.

ROISIN: Good for you Bernadette, have you taken many?

BERNIE: Well, I've ...

ALEX: Thirty-eight!

BERNIE: Twenty-eight. I'm hopin' to take my test soon.

ALEX: Oh, she's doin' well. Only last week she pulled away from our front door and run into the back of an army saracen. The instructor went mad. He asked why she didn't luck in the mirror. She said she did. But that she'd left her glasses in the house.

ROISIN: Those driving schools used to use this street all the time, until Bill and the Association got it stopped.

BILL: It was getting ridiculous—non-stop traffic.

ALEX: How did you get it stopped?

BILL: Oh, by simply using the array of people we have living in the street, and one or two other contacts.

ROISIN: We've two or three top civil servants in this street.

BILL: One Judge, one Crown Prosecutor.

ROISIN: One ex-Lord Mayor.

BILL: We have some City Hall heavyweights on our side.

ROISIN: And our MP is a barrister friend of Bill's, that helps too.

BERNIE: Judges, Lord Mayors—in our street?

ALEX: Lot a good contacts there. A hope some of then can help me.

BILL: In what direction? [ALEX *hands out cigarettes as he explains.*]

ALEX: Well, I've just bought premises on the main road up there and a've put in for plannin' permission.

ROISIN: You're opening a restaurant?

IGNATIUS: Nouvelle cuisine.

ALEX: Ach, it's nothin' much.

BILL: Really Alex, any kind of commercial development in this vicinity is rather frowned upon by the Association. It is a residential area.

ALEX: It's only a oul' hamburger carry-out place. There's none up this way.

BILL: A hamburger place?

BERNIE: We'll be selling squid and prawns.

[*The Blakelys smile at each other uncomfortably.*]

BILL: You could run into one or two problems.

ROISIN: Oh, I don't know, it might work out alright.

BILL: There'll be opposition.

ALEX: Well, we'll see. More drinks?

ROISIN: Yes, I'll have one.

ALEX: Bill?

BILL: None for me, thanks.

JAN: I'm okay.

[ALEX *serves* ROISIN *and* BERNIE *drinks.* JAN *is bored by the proceedings except on the occasions when she looks to find* IGNATIUS *is looking at her.*]

ALEX: You're not goin, Bill?

BILL: Oh, we've an early start in the mornin'.

ALEX: I didn't know solicitors worked on Saturday mornings.

ROISIN: Oh, he's not working. We're off to London on the 8.30 shuttle.

ALEX: Very nice.

BERNIE: Visit your sister?

ROISIN: We usually do call in to see Emer, but we'll be awfully busy. I'll be shopping for some clothes on Saturday—I really do need some new clothes—we'll be visiting the Tate Gallery and the British Museum on Sunday and then, the real purpose for our trip is on Monday—Sothebys. You know, the auctions?

BERNIE: Oh yes.

ROISIN: Bill has bought some marvellous paintings at Sothebys. And only last year, Bernadette, I bought the most beautiful old Chinese porcelain. But this time it's Bill who's bidding. He's chasing a Lowry.

BERNIE: A lorry?

ROISIN: Lowry. You know, the Manchester painter. He was only an ordinary working man, a mere rent collector.

ALEX [*singing*]: 'He painted matchstick men and matchstick cats and dogs.'

ROISIN: You know him, Alex?

ALEX: Only through the song.

BILL: Roisin, I am not chasing a Lowry. Do you know how much a Lowry goes for nowadays?

ROISIN: I think he was a fake.

BILL: Don't start that again, Roisin.

ROISIN: He was!

BILL: He wasn't!

ROISIN: Look. It's exactly the same as Peter Brook's production of Carmen in Paris. Because the critics raved over it, you raved over it. I did not like the Paris production Bill, and I don't like Lowry, I'm sorry.

BERNIE: Do you mean t'say that ... that you went all the way to Paris to see a play?

ROISIN: No, not really. We actually went for the Arc de Triomphe—you know the horse race—and we managed to get tickets for Carmen in the evening, so we were really lucky. And you'll never guess who was sitting at the next table to us in the restaurant afterwards?

ALEX: General de Gaulle?

ROISIN: Lester Pigott! He was riding in the race.

ALEX: You should have hit him a good dig in the bake.

ROISIN: Why?

ALEX: For all the money I've threw away on the bastard.

BERNIE: Alex!

BILL: Look. [*Looking at his watch*] We really must be going. It's been really nice meeting you.

ROISIN: It was lovely. Thank you for inviting us in.

BERNIE: Not a'tall, our pleasure.

BILL: Right. Look—[*Handing* ALEX *some leaflets*]—I'd like you to read some of this. It's really only some information bumph from the Association. That one's the constitution. I'm sorry if it seems rather formal. And that one has all the latest bridge info.

ROISIN: I hope you'll have a game, Bernadette?

BERNIE: God a couldn't. At school I never got beyond long division.

BILL: And this one's our latest leaflet on 'Defecating on the Street'.

ALEX: Don't tell me yiz have a problem in this district with people—

BILL: No, no, dogs.

ROISIN: It's a big issue in London at the moment.

BERNIE: Anything we can do to help Mr. Blakely, you don't have to ask, just say. Isn't that right Alex?

ALEX: Yes, certainly, anything a'tall.

BILL: Right, we'll be off.

ALEX: See yiz later.

[*The Blakelys move to exit but* ROISIN *attracts Bill's attention*]

BILL: Oh, nearly forgot. We're having dinner in our house Friday week. Nothing special, just ourselves and the Association secretary, Mr. Conerney and his wife. We would be delighted if you would join us?

BERNIE: We'd love to.

ROISIN: Say ... 7.30?

ALEX: No problem.

BILL: Good. We'll see you then, Friday week.

[*At this* JULIA *enters wearing only her bra and knickers and carrying an empty glass. Still half-asleep and without a word to anybody she lifts a bottle of sherry out of the box and exits through another door. Everyone stares after her.*]

BILL: Right, see you Friday week?

ALEX: Friday week.

BERNIE: Cheerio now.

ROISIN: Bye.

[IGNATIUS *winks at* JAN *and the* BLAKELYS *exit.*]

ALEX: Isn't it as well she had her bra and knickers on?

SCENE 5

The Blakely garden. JAN *is planting seeds in a tray of soil.* IGNATIUS *enters.*

IGGY: Hiya.

JAN: Hiya.

IGGY: What are you doin'?

JAN: Growing hybrid marijuana, what do you think.

IGNATIUS [*very interested*]: Serious?

JAN: Wise. I'm planting artichokes.

IGNATIUS: Jerusalem, Chinese or Globe?

JAN: Belfast ones actually. Ever grow them?

IGNATIUS: Not a'tall. Wouldn't lower myself to grow 'vegetables'.

JAN: Why not?

IGNATIUS: I prefer to grow flowers. Beautiful things. Ever seen a rhododendron in full bloom?

JAN: You can't eat rhododendrons.

IGNATIUS: Depends what part of the body you want to feed. If you knew anything about these things, which you obviously don't, you'd know that the main diet of the Chinese is boiled rice and rhododendrons.

JAN: Your head's a stethescope.

IGNATIUS: It's true. Y'see it all goes back to a wee man called Chu Ling who lived hundreds of years ago in a wee village called Chatee awayyyyy up in the very tip-top of Northern China—know like on the border with Russia.

Well, wee Chu was a gardener for a big noble family and his favourite plant was the rhododendron. So, he planted the bastards everywhere, so much so that within twenty years the whole shebang was covered in red rhoddys.

Anyway, one particular winter turned out to be the worst in livin' memory. People were kickin' the bucket all over the show, the livestock was disappearin' as fast as whales off the Japanese coast and all the crops were totally banjaxed. It was the pits. So bad in fact that, Chu Ling's boss actually spoke to him. He said, 'Chu?' Chu said, 'What boss?' Nigh like, in Chinese. His boss said, 'Chu, this is terrible weather.' Chu said, 'Fuckin' despert, Boss.' Anyway, by spring the weather was still atrocious. People still keelin' over, livestock still bitin' the dust, there wasn't a bite to eat anywhere when booooooooommm—this massive storm broke out.

It was fierce. Hundred mile an hour winds, raindrops so big the would knock a feg outta your mouth—I mean it was fierce. Everybody was runnin' to the chemist for valium when suddenly—[*Makes a sharp whistle and slices his hand across thin air*]—just as quick as it had come, it stopped.

Just like that—stop.

And quicker than it takes to say 'two beef curries with fried rice and a spring roll'—the sun was out, blazin'. Red hot. Nobody had ever clapped their mince-pies on anything like it.

But then, suddenly, somebody noticed something very strange—probably a nosy oul' git—suddenly this nosy oul' git noticed that all the rhododendrons were in full bloom. Every bush every single bud. They weren't supposed to come out until June. So people put two and two together and worked out that wee Chu Ling's rhododendrons had stopped the storm.

So. From that day on the red rhoddy of the Tahe province became famous throughout China as a symbol of luck and good fortune. So when I heard we were movin' up to this godforsaken part of the world I got one for our garden. Kindly donated by the Department of Parks & Cemeteries.

JAN: Good story. Where did you get all this knowledge of plants?

IGNATIUS: Work. I'm a gardener in Musgrave Park. But I go to night-classes too.

JAN: Horticulture.

IGNATIUS: Naa. 'A' levels—Sociology and English.

JAN: To become what?

IGNATIUS: You mean besides rich and famous? What I really wanna be is a singer/songwriter. Ever hear of Sam Cooke?

JAN: Did he live down by Sandy Row?

IGNATIUS: No, y'bleep ye. Sam Cooke was a black singer/songwriter from the 1960s. He was shot dead in a row over a white prostitute.

JAN: And you wanna be shot dead over a white prostitute?

IGNATIUS: No, the first bit—singer/songwriter.

JAN: If you're gonna dream, dream big.

IGNATIUS: What about you?

JAN: I've been doing medicine for four years.

IGNATIUS: Did a judge hand that out?

JAN: It's not quite that bad.

IGNATIUS: Up to your oxters in blood for the rest of your life.

JAN: Depends what area you specialise in.

IGNATIUS: What do you fancy?

JAN: I think I'll go for gynae.

IGNATIUS: Women's parts?

JAN: Or obstetrics.

IGNATIUS: Or what?

JAN: Delivering babies. Or I might become a plumber.

IGNATIUS: A plumber?

JAN: Urology. Matters relating to the kidney, bladder et cetera.

IGNATIUS: Yucckk. Y'might as well be a lavatory attendant.

JAN: Sometimes it feels like that. I don't even know if I really wanna do medicine.

IGNATIUS: Why did y'choose it?

JAN: Dunno. But Mum and Dad have always been on to me to get to university and get a profession. [IGNATIUS *is smiling.*] What's wrong?

IGNATIUS: Just thinkin' about the difference between your house and mine. On my 16th birthday m'ma stopped the washin' machine for a minute and made a long, eloquent, caring speech about my future.

JAN: What did she say?

IGNATIUS: 'Hey boy, you're 16 nigh so get up off your arse and go out and find a job.' I said, 'Ma, can I not go to university?' Sh'said,

'A'll put m'toe up your arse, if y'don't go out and bring some money into this house.' Your ma and da were debatin' whether you should be a doctor or a solicitor, while my ma was debatin' how far my first wages were gonna spread. But it's different nigh.

JAN: Stop saying 'nigh'.

IGNATIUS: Whadaya want me t'say?

JAN: Speak properly.

IGNATIUS: Like you?

JAN: I use the English Language.

IGNATIUS: Tell me—apart from BBC newsreaders and the Royal Family—who actually uses standard English?

JAN: A lot of people ...

IGNATIUS: Hobby horses crap. Standard English is borin' and restricted. My mates use the English language the way a fashion designer approaches a new dress. Drop a bit here, add this on, turn that round—changin' it all the time. It's ordinary people who keep the English language a livin' language. Give is a word?

JAN: What?

IGNATIUS: Just say the first word that comes into your head and I'll give you five different words for it.

JAN: Am ... tray.

IGNATIUS [*stuck*]: No well .... give is another one.

JAN: Drunk.

IGNATIUS: Steamboats, airlocked, bluttered, oiled, watered, blotto— give me a kiss?

JAN: What?

IGNATIUS: A kiss. I know you well over five minutes now.

JAN: You must be joking. [IGNATIUS *leans forward and steals a longish kiss.*] If you ever do that again I'll report you under the Fair Trading and Descriptions Act. I've had better kisses from my pet budgie. Tray please? [IGNATIUS *hands her the second tray.*]

IGNATIUS: So your da's a solicitor?

JAN: Yep.

IGNATIUS: Are you a Prod or a Taig?

JAN: None of your business.

IGNATIUS: Come on, what are you?

JAN: I'm Baha'i.

IGNATIUS: Yes, but are you a Protestant Baha'i or a Catholic Baha'i?

JAN: Don't be silly.

IGNATIUS: So what is it? Do you have to be a vegetarian, sandal-wearin' hippy?

JAN: It's nothing of the sort. Baha'i is a universal religion that believes in peace and happiness. And—it's as far away from Catholics and Protestants as I could get.

IGNATIUS: Okay, what are your parents?

JAN: For a start they're not my parents. Not my real parents. I'm adopted. He's a good Prod and mum's a mad Catholic.

IGNATIUS: Join the club.

JAN: Really?

IGNATIUS: Yeah. Bernie's a half-nun and Alex's a top UVF man. Usual sort of Belfast marriage. Plus Alex is only m'step da.

JAN: I'm not the only one with complications?

IGNATIUS: Complications? Bahai? If you wanted t'die for Ireland, the wouldn't let you. You couldn't even kick football for Linfield Football Club.

JAN: Well, the good thing around here is that no one bothers about religion.

IGNATIUS: They're all atheists?

JAN: No. They're all very religious but they keep it to themselves.

IGNATIUS: Very civilised.

JAN: Bigotry doesn't pay among the well-heeled.

IGNATIUS: Frig, down our way, there's one street separates us and even if a Protestant dog crossed it, the Catholics would be out in their hundreds shoutin' 'Tiochaidh Ar La!' Down our way we would fight over the colour of the kerbstones.

JAN: Up here, the only thing they'll fight over is the colour of money.

IGNATIUS [*suddenly distracted*]: Frig me, there's our dogs on the loose!

JAN [*both standing*]: Where?

IGNATIUS: There! [*Pointing*] Chasin' that woman up her back garden! Come on! [*They rush off.*]

JAN: That's Mrs. Conerney!

SCENE 6

BILL BLAKELY *and* EAMONN CONERNEY *on the phone.* BILL *is dressed in best suit etc.* EAMONN *is half-way through the process of dressing, and is clearly agitated.*

EAMONN: Bill?

BILL: Yes, Eamonn?

EAMONN: Can't make the dinner tonight.

BILL: What's the problem?

EAMONN: It's those McFadden dogs again.

BILL: What happened?

EAMONN: I'm going to have to sue.

BILL: Sue?

EAMONN: Lynda was taking in some washing tonight when one of them bit her—on the left buttock. [BILL *laughs.*] Neither of us found it remotely amusing, Bill.

BILL: Sorry, Eamonn ...

EAMONN: You'll have to have a word with them—those bloody dogs will have to be put down.

BILL: Then you'll have to be here.

EAMONN: I can't. I'm waiting on the doctor.

BILL: Look, we had it arranged to confront them tonight, remember?

EAMONN: I'd rather just leave it to the police.

BILL: I agree, but we have a responsibility to personally represent the Association. You must come over, Eamonn.

EAMONN: Yes, yes, alright.

BILL: Don't forget your list of complaints from the Association and I have the documentation re: the hamburger joint.

EAMONN: Alright I'll come over. I take it you've heard about the donkey?

BILL: Donkey?

EAMONN: They have a donkey.

BILL: I don't believe you.

EAMONN: Lynda saw a donkey being delivered this afternoon.

BILL: You *better* come over then, we'll have plenty to tell them.

EAMONN: Plenty to tell them! I've had to get the doctor out to examine my wife's arse! [EAMONN *slams the phone down.*]

SCENE 7

ROISIN *and* ALEX *enter the Blakely drawing-room, glasses of wine in hand.* ROISIN *is wearing a swish evening dress while* ALEX *is wearing a yellow tracksuit.*

ALEX: I was brought up Church of Ireland, m'da fell out with the Minister and w'went Baptist. Then we moved to the new estate where there was only one place of worship so we went over to the

Methodists. Then m'da was caught with his fingers in the Methodist collection plate and we went back to the Church of Ireland. Apart from that like, we were always good Protestants.

ROISIN: If you'd said to me, Alex, when I was twenty that I was going to marry a Protestant, I'd have laughed at you. In fact my father did laugh at me. He threw me out. But then when they realised Bill was so well off—well, everything changed. He can do no wrong now.

ALEX: Aye, Bernie hesitated with me for a while ... know 'cause, like, I was in the Orange Order, I've a brother even doin' time for the UVF. Bernie said I was from a 'hardline loyalist' family and that it would never work out between us. Then one day by accident she read my bank statement and I'm tellin' ye boy, I coulda been the Officer Commanding the UVF and she'da still married me.

ROISIN: That's a terrible thing to say.

ALEX [*chuckles*]: Yeah, I'm only jokin'. Salt of the good earth is Bernie. Ah'll never forget the night a met her. She was singin' in the Rocktown Bar. I always remember what she sang that night, 'Foolish Heart'. Y'know that one ... [*He sings a few lines quickly*] 'The night is like a lovely tune, beware my foolish heart, and like the everlasting moon ...'? I fell for Bernie right from the minute she started singin' that song. She has a beautiful voice, y'know. You should come down to the Rocktown sometime, Roisin—you and Bill—it's a smashin' singsong. Me and Bernie goes every Saturday night.

ROISIN: That would be nice. Where is it?

ALEX: Down the Docks. [ROISIN *almost chokes on her drink*]

ROISIN: Yes, I must mention it to Bill.

ALEX: Like it's non-sectarian. All sorts goes. That's one good thing about drink—it affects us all the same way. Catholic or Protestant, middle-class or working-class, man or woman—we all know what it's like to boke all over the bedroom floor after too much drink.

ROISIN: Yes, yes indeed.

ALEX: Come to mention it. This wine's very nice.

ROISIN: Do you like it?

ALEX: Beautiful.

ROISIN: That'll please Bill. He's just bought two cases of it.

ALEX: Oh, do you buy in bulk? I've a mate, Big Trevor, he deals in drink, he might be able to get you it cheap. Big Trevor has contacts in all the major distributors—that's the people that supplies the off-licences.

ROISIN: There's not much in an off-licence that would interest Bill. He has it shipped in from London on special order.

ALEX: Direct to the house?

ROISIN: Right to the front door.

[BILL *enters in best suit etc. and carrying a glass and a bottle of wine.*]

BILL: Everyone got drinks?

ROISIN: Yes fine.

ALEX: Dead on, Bill.

BILL: How do you like that wine, Alex?

ALEX: I was just sayin' to Roisin there, tastes a bit like vinegar. [BILL *is aghast.*] M'only jokin'. Very nice, Bill. And the meal was terrific too. Thanks.

ROISIN: Thank you.

BILL: Except Roisin didn't cook it. [ALEX *looks quizzically.*]

ROISIN: Caterers.

BILL: Expensive caterers.

ROISIN: But well worth it.

ALEX: Jasis, don't be tellin' the Lady Mayoress, she'll be wantin' caterers in every night. She's already conplainin' that with her night-classes and everything she's no time for things like cookin'.

BILL: She does night-classes?

ALEX: English Literature, English Language and Knittin'.

ROISIN: Very good for her.

ALEX: The Bladonmore's Road's doin' a lot for my Bernie. And night-classes is only the start.

BILL: I think it's very commendable for a woman of Bernadette's ... background.

ROISIN: Super—for a woman of Bernadette's age to ...

[BERNIE *enters wearing a matching yellow track-suit.*]

BERNIE [*normal accent, sternly*]: What was that about my age?

ROISIN: I was just saying how full of life and vitality you are.

BERNIE: Oh I always put that down to the good, healthy upbringing my mother and father gave us.

ALEX; Aye, a plate a champ every day and twice a day at weekends.

[IGNATIUS *and* JAN *enter downstage, outdoors.* JAN *runs on and* IGNATIUS *catches her. They giggle and grapple, then embrace and kiss passionately.*]

ROISIN: Our Jan is doing Medicine at Queen's. She's going to be a gynaecologist.

BERNIE: Like your man ... David Bellamy?

ROISIN: Not exactly. But just recently, Bill and I have become just a little concerned. She has been going rather too steadily with a boyfriend.

ALEX: Girls will be girls.

BILL: Oh, Ronnie's a nice enough chap, Roisin.

ROISIN: I know he is. His father's well-off, in property and all that, and the boy works for his father, but I'd rather she waited before getting too involved. I think her education comes first, Bernadette, don't you?

BERNIE: Definitely. And the young fellas that's knocking about now.

[IGNATIUS *and* JAN *run across the stage again and kiss and cuddle.*]

ROISIN: I wouldn't trust any young fella these days.

BERNIE: Oh, I've warned my Antionette—keep your distance.

[*At this* JULIA *enters downstage, outdoors. She is drunk and singing* 'Your Good Girl's Gonna Go Bad'. *She stops to take a nip of drink she has in her handbag. Resumes singing—louder.*]

BILL: Good God, what could that be?

ROISIN: Sounds like someone ... drunk!

BILL: Couldn't be.

ROISIN: It is.

[JULIA *rings their doorbell.*]

ALEX [*nearest*]: I'll get it.

BERNIE: Don't.

ALEX: It's alright, I'll get it. [*He opens the door.*]

JULIA [*entering*]: For a minute there, a thought a was in the wrong house.

BERNIE [*normal accent, stern*]: It is the wrong house!

JULIA: Oh look. Mary Peters and Sebastian Coe. [*To* BILL] You're a fine luckin' big man. What's your name?

BERNIE: What are you doin' here?

JULIA: What am a doin' here? A'm lucky a got here. A musta rapped every fuckin' door in the street.

BERNIE [*affected accent*]: Sorry about this, Roisin.

JULIA: Not a one opened their door.

BILL [*looking at watch*]: Probably terrified.

JULIA: Right Alex son, what about a wee glass a confidence?

[BERNIE *moves towards her.*]

BERNIE [*normal accent*]: I'll confidence ye. Come on t'hell a that w'ye. B'Jasis you're standin' there like the last whore of Babylon. [*Takes her by the arm to the door*]

JULIA: You never introduced me—

[*Outside*]

BERNIE: Introduce ye? You're lucky I don't brain ye, makin' a showbox of yourself there. [JULIA *moves off.*] There's our house

[*Pointing*] and see if you waken wee Julie Lorenzia ...

[EAMONN CONERNEY *enters and passes* JULIA *and* BERNIE, *staring as he goes*]

BERNIE [*affected accent*]: Beautiful evening, isn't it.

JULIA: Who's he? He looks like he's got a glyserine sypository stuck up his arse.

[EAMONN *walks on past, bewildered, into the Blakely home.*]

BERNIE [*shouting*]: Y'may book into the Salvation Army first thing in the mornin'.

[BERNIE *turns back inside.* JULIA *exits. Downstage* JAN *and* IGNATIUS *are kissing.* JULIA *arrives beside them.*]

JULIA: Would ya luck at this. *Lady Chatterley's Lover* all over again.

IGNATIUS: Julia, you're back.

JULIA: What's wrong with my back?

IGNATIUS: C'mon d'we get you home.

[*They exit together. Meanwhile, back at the Blakelys.*]

BILL: Alex, there's no need to take this personally.

ALEX: He insulted my wife.

EAMONN: I'm stating facts.

BERNIE [*normal accent*]: Are you tryin' to say I'm a bad mother?

ROISIN: I don't think Eamonn meant that, Bernadette.

EAMONN: Mrs. McFadden, your Camillus has caused chaos since the first day he arrived on this street.

ALEX: Y'still haven't told us what he's done.

EAMONN: Alright, I'll tell you. [*Refers to sheet of paper*] Friday—Seized his dogs on Mrs. Spotswood and Mrs. Archard. Saturday—Broke into Rutherford Graham's garage and painted, 'F— the Grahams' on the garage wall.

BERNIE: Wrong. My Camillus's not allowed to use bad language.

EAMONN: I could show you the wall, Mrs. McFadden.

BERNIE: Whada I wanna luck at a wall for?

EAMONN: Sunday—Camillus ran up and down the Bladonmore Road without his trousers on. When approached by Mrs Hall-Hamilton, he shook his private parts at her.

[ALEX *finds it difficult not to laugh.*]

BERNIE: Sunday was a very warm day.

EAMONN: Tuesday—broke into Mr. McCleave's car—the former Lord Mayor—and wrote 'Madonna is a Ride' all over the seats.

BERNIE: He does like Madonna, like, I know that nigh.

EAMONN: And yesterday. He burned down Pascal McGreevey's garden shed.

ALEX: He denies that.

BERNIE: Mr. McGreevy's son admitted lightin' the match.

EAMONN: Yes, but your Camillus had the McGreevey pet rabbit over at the garden pool and was holding it's head under the water until young Patrick agreed to burn down his own father's garden shed. And there's the dog's attack tonight on my wife.

BERNIE: My Camillus never behaved like this in our old district.

EAMONN: What do you mean by that?

BERNIE: A mean it's only since he started chummin' with your son and the other wee lads fron this street! This street's a bad influence on him.

ROISIN: I think that's a rather unfair allegation, Bernadette.

EAMONN: There's also the question of this donkey.

ALEX: What about the donkey?

BILL: You must agree Alex, the idea—

ALEX: Agree nothin'. The donkey was bought for Camillus's birthday. He stays in my back garden and does nobody any harm, right.

EAMONN: What are you going to do about the dogs?

ALEX: We'll ah ... we'll get muzzles for them.

BERNIE: We're gettin' a box for them.

EAMONN: Okay Bill, the premises.

BILL: Yes Alex, about your application for planning permission to open a Hot Food Bar on the front of the road.

ALEX: What about it?

EAMONN: It won't be happening.

ALEX: What won't?

BILL: The Residents' Association held a meeting and we are unanimously opposed to the idea. We want to keep the area residential.

ALEX: And I wanna earn a livin'.

EAMONN: We have lodged 22 different objections with the Town Clerk.

BILL: The present Lord Mayor has agreed to support our case.

EAMONN: Out of the seven councillors on the Town Planning Committee, we believe we have the support of five.

ALEX: This sounds like the Mafia.

ROISIN: We have to protect our environment.

BERNIE: But there is no carry-out place up round here.

EAMONN: We can do without a hamburger joint.

BERNIE: I'll have you know, we're gonna sell—

ALEX: Leave it, Bernie. I think a have the general picture nigh. Come on, we're goin'.

BILL: As I said Alex, there's nothing whatsoever personal about this. We're just representing the interests of the street.

ALEX: Aye, well, we live in the street too. [*They move to exit.*]

BERNIE: And in case you didn't know, mister, we're gonna sell caviar and lobster soup! [*They exit and stop outside.*]

ALEX: One correction, Bernie love. We *were* goin' to sell caviar and lobster soup.

BERNIE: We *are*.

ALEX: They've blocked us.

BERNIE: Have the? I might've been brought up in a poor area but there's one thing that taught me—how to fight. And I'm gonna fight the Bladonmore Road every inch of the way. Right?

ALEX: Right, love.

BERNIE: Just one thing.

ALEX: What's that?

BERNIE: When the Blakelys came to our house for a drink they wore tracksuits and we were all dressed up.

ALEX: Right.

BERNIE: Nigh, when we visit their house and went out and bought tracksuits and every friggin' thing—they were all dressed up! [*Moving to exit*] Bloody odd, aren't the? I don't know what way the live up here, a'tall do you? From nigh on, we'll just be ourselves. [*They exit.*]

Black-out

ACT TWO

SCENE 1

The McFadden living-room. It is cluttered with boxes of food and catering-size bottles of sauce etc. ALEX *and* IGNATIUS *are checking the stock.*

ALEX: Doesn't seem t'be any scampi.

IGNATIUS: M'ma's gettin' them outta the big freezer.

ALEX: Right, that seems to be the lot. Hamburgers, baps, sausages, eggs, relish, thousand island, tartar sauce, salad cream, lettuce, tomatoes ...

IGNATIUS [*joking*]: But no lobster soup.

ALEX: Keep your fingers crossed, a think she has forgot. Right. So I'm doin' the general Bladonmore Road area, up as far as—

IGNATIUS: Are y'sure you're gonna get away with this, Alex?

ALEX: 'Course! I've got the temporary street-tradin' licence—and while they hold back our plannin' permission—we bring the food to the people. That was very good of your man to sell is the hamburger van for five hundred quid, wasn't it?

IGNATIUS: Aye, especially after Big Trevor punched him.

ALEX: 'Course, ideally I would need two vans—just to rub it into these bastards—but in the meantime, your ma and Julya will have to make do with the Hot Food Trailer. Only cost me twenty quid.

IGNATIUS: After Big Trevor attempted to rip the man's arm from its socket.

ALEX: A'm puttin' the trailer at the end of this street—that way the whole district'll know we're here quicker than it takes them to switch on their Aga cookers. I don't think we have enough lettuce.

IGNATIUS: And we need some new videos.

ALEX: What?

IGNATIUS: Some videos—for watchin' later on—know like, the ones you've been gettin'.

112

ALEX: I haven't been gettin' any videos.

IGNATIUS: Come on Alex. Last week it was *Debbie Goes To Dallas*—this week it's *Danish Nurses On Parade*—think I don't know?

[ALEX *looks around guiltily, lowers his voice and points at* IGNATIUS.]

ALEX: Listen hey boy! Don't you be tellin' your ma anything about this.

IGNATIUS: Much is it worth?

ALEX: Ignatius son, there's things woman don't understand about men. We're two very different species. Men like lookin' at women's bodies and women like candlelit dinners. That's the way it is.

[BERNIE *enters, carrying packets of frozen prawns.*]

BERNIE: Do y'know what I forgot?

ALEX: No, what?

BERNIE: The lobster soup!

ALEX: Bernie love, y'only get lobster soup in the very, very, very best of high-class establishments—you'll be sittin' in a Hot Food Trailer in the street.

BERNIE: Who's doin' the trailer with me?

ALEX: Julya.

BERNIE: Julya? My God! Sure isn't this her night for the Rocktown?

ALEX: She's off the drink, isn't she.

IGNATIUS: That's right. She hasn't had a drink for over two weeks. She said she'd rather take disinfectant than take another solitary drink.

ALEX: And I think she's done well.

BERNIE: Where is she anyway?

IGNATIUS: Upstairs gettin' ready. She says it'll be cold so she's puttin' on plenty of winter woolies.

BERNIE: Ignatius, you're not goin' out!

IGNATIUS: I didn't say a was.

BERNIE: No, that chile's t'be minded.

IGNATIUS: Jan's comin' over to babysit with me.

[BERNIE *glares at him accusingly.*]

BERNIE: I don't want no more trouble over that chile. Imagine! A social worker comin' to my door because Ralph—sleaked-arse Ralph—complained that Julie Lorenzia was bein' neglected. Imagine!

ALEX: Bernie, you know the chile's well lucked after.

BERNIE: Lucked after? She's gettin' a better rearin' than the Last Emperor of China.

IGNATIUS: It's all just part of their campaign to force us out.

BERNIE: They've about as much chance of forcin' me outta here as Julya has of gettin' Mickey Kelly to kiss her.

IGNATIUS: But they're tryin' hard enough. Right down to sendin' a solicitor's letter about the donkey.

ALEX: Sure what about the night the sent the cops here over the 'loud music'. Julya was playin' Perry Como!

IGNATIUS: And it was definitely the Association was behind Camillus' new Headmaster comin' to the house yesterday.

ALEX: I told him not to bring that donkey to school.

BERNIE: His school chums wanted to see it.

ALEX: Then there's the summons over Conerney's wife's arse.

IGNATIUS: We're only here three months and they've tried every trick in the book.

ALEX: The definitely have a high opinion of themselves.

BERNIE: So had Idi Amin and luck what happened t'him.

ALEX: Well, I've done a wee bit of m'own investigatin' and there's not too many of them has any cause t'be high and mighty.

BERNIE: Whadaya mean?

ALEX: Your man Bill. Our next-door-neighbour Bill, the same man who came into our house and welcomed us to the Bladonmore Road? He's a crook.

BERNIE: I knew—thon fella has eyes that would open a padlock.

ALEX: And our friend O.P. Conerney the Builder? He's about as honest as John DeLorean.

IGNATIUS: How do y'know?

ALEX: How? I've had my spies out. You name it. Every trick in the book. Young Eamonn's particulary well-known for the money he spends on Buildin' Inspectors.

IGNATIUS: He's into bribery?

BERNIE: But he's a Catholic.

ALEX: I've tried to tell you before Bernie love, bein' a member of St. Vincent de Paul does not make people perfect.

BERNIE: I suppose not. But they've no call to start actin' like Protestants.

ALEX: Bernie dear, did you know that Martin Luther jacked in the Catholic Church because he said it was corrupt?

BERNIE: Sure how could you take the word of a Protestant?

ALEX: He wasn't a Protestant at the time! Ach, it doesn't matter. What I'm sayin' is, Eamonn Conerney is corrupt. When his work isn't up to standard the Buildin' Inspectors get backhanders all round.

BERNIE: God, you'd meet more decent men at a Convention of Child Molesters.

ALEX: Yes. Our respectable friends, who luck down on *us*, would be more or less among friends at a Welcome Home party for the Kray twins.

IGNATIUS: There's such a thin line between business and robbery.

ALEX: Hey boyyyyyy!

IGNATIUS: As Brendan Behan says, 'Sure what's a crook only a businessman without a shop.'

BERNIE: Ignatius son, crooks end up in jail, respectable businesspeople do not.

IGNATIUS: Exactly. Our jails are filled with the workin'-classes, while the establishment lives by the eleventh commandment—'The Rich Shall Not Go To Jail.'

ALEX: Let's keep our fingers crossed.

BERNIE: All's I know is we all have to get money from somewhere.

IGNATIUS: Spot on, ma. Lend is a fiver?

BERNIE: What do you need five pounds for?

IGNATIUS: I wanna join the Freemasons. Learn how to stay outta jail.

BERNIE: Ignatius son, you're about as funny as an operation for piles. Here.

ALEX: A'd say the oul' off-licence'll get a touch.

BERNIE: Well dar he. [BERNIE *gives him the money. At this,* JAN *arrives.*]

JAN: Hello everybody. [*The others greet her.*] Oh, congratulations Mrs. McFadden on passing your driving test today. I heard you did very well.

ALEX: Oh, *she* did very well okay, but the poor examiner had to take the rest of the day off sufferin' from loose bowels.

BERNIE: Thanks very much, Jan. We're havin' a wee celebration drink later on. Maybe you and Ignatius would—

IGNATIUS: Actually ma, there was something we were wantin' to ask you.

BERNIE: We? Is that wee girl in trouble?

IGNATIUS: Wise. It's just Jan wants to come over.

BERNIE: What?

IGNATIUS: Defect.

BERNIE: D'what?

IGNATIUS: She was wantin' to know if she could move in with us?

BERNIE: In the name a God!

JAN: I need to get away from them, Mrs. McFadden.

ALEX: What? By movin' next door?

JAN: It's gettin' worse every day. Everything they do to you, I get more and more ashamed of them. Their behaviour has been nothing short of insidious.

BERNIE [*unsure*]: Well ... a wouldn't say they've been ... that.

IGNATIUS: Can she stay?

BERNIE: A suppose ... a few nights.

JAN: Oh thank you, Mrs. McFadden.

IGNATIUS: Great! [*Rubbing his hands*]

BERNIE: She's not stayin' in your room!

ALEX: Right. Nigh that we have an extra chef joinin' the staff, let's get out and bring our 'International Cuisine' to the people. Ignatius, start loadin' up.

IGNATIUS: Right, Bladonmore Road here they come.

ALEX [*to* JAN *and* BERNIE]: C'mon you two, give is a hand out with this stuff? [*Much activity*]

BERNIE: Hold on, hold on, where the hell's Julya?

[JULIA *enters from the stairs dressed in a French maid's outfit, mini-skirt, high-heels etc.*]

JULIA. A'm comin, a'm comin.

BERNIE: Ah, Holy Mary and Saint Bernadette, luck who it is—Betty Grable.

ALEX: Julya, y'luck immaculate.

JULIA: Thank you, Alex. There's no good goin' out t'sell hot dogs unless y'luck the part.

BERNIE: A don't mind y'luckin' the part, but nobody said anything about luckin' like a tart! C'mon.

IGNATIUS: Aunt Julya, at least you'll attract the male customers.

BERNIE: The only thing she'll attract is the Vice Squad.

[*The others busy themselves and exit while* BERNIE *approaches* IGNATIUS.]

BERNIE: And c'mere you heyboy. You listen for that chile.

IGNATIUS: What chile? [BERNIE *glares.*] Oh, y'mean the chocolate factory.

BERNIE: And another thing. See your man Brutus that makes the speech—'I love Caesar but I had to kill him'. Why the hell does he say a stupid thing like that?

IGNATIUS: No ma, what he actually says is, 'Not that I loved Caesar less but that I loved Rome more.' He was doin' it for his country.

BERNIE: Murderin' for his country? B'Jasis Rome musta had as many buck-eejits as we have.

SCENE 2

The Blakely Home. BILL, ROISIN and EAMONN CONERNEY *in evening dress, are preparing to leave.* BILL *is shining his shoes while* ROISIN *puts the last touches to her eyes.* EAMONN *is agitated.*

EAMONN: But they've already gone too far, Bill.

BILL: He who loses his head loses the fight.

EAMONN: I'm not losing my head.

BILL: You're practically frothing at the mouth.

EAMONN: I am not. I'm merely telling you that the entire street has had enough. The McFaddens have to go—now!

BILL: We do not, as yet, have powers of eviction.

ROISIN: I don't believe I've ever come across a more uncouth family.

EAMONN: I still say we should arrive at their door—in deputation— and simply ask them to sell up.

BILL: Look, Eamonn. I know these sort of people. I worked on building sites in my student days and I see them coming up before the courts. I know the mentality. And I assure you—give them just a little more time, a little more rope—they'll hang their good selves soon enough.

EAMONN: How long are we prepared to wait? Until the price of our houses starts to fall?

ROISIN: Till that ... monster of a boy, Camillus, does serious damage to one of our children?

EAMONN: Maybe you want to wait, Bill, until it's not just a donkey and two dogs they have out the back but a bloody zoo!

ROISIN: I was talking to Emer on the phone last night about the donkey dirtying in our driveway and she says that if that happened in London, the Council would prosecute immediately. Bill, hurry up.

EAMONN: I think they should be locked up.

ROISIN: I'm beginning to agree.

BILL: Look, we've done everything we need to do, up as far as this point.

EAMONN: What about selective internment?

BILL: We've effectively put an end to his Fish & Chip shop on the front of the road. We've kept the police fully informed of every single indiscretion committed. It's really only a matter, Eamonn, of turning the screw—slowly but surely. Where's my coat, dear?

ROISIN: In the bedroom.

EAMONN: What about the house parties every weekend and that woman, Julia, screetching at the top of her voice?

BILL: I rather enjoy her interpretation of 'So Deep Is The Night'.

[BILL *exits.* ROISIN *approaches* EAMONN.]

ROISIN: Don't get too upset. It's Prize night at the Club remember? We're supposed to enjoy ourselves.

EAMONN [*forcing a smile*]: Yes, you're right. [*He kisses her briefly on the forehead.*]

ROISIN: And my husband is making a speech as the new Captain.

EAMONN [*sarcastically*]: I know.

ROISIN: And you are Golfer of the Year.

EAMONN [*smugly*]: Again.

[*They hear Bill approaching and move away from each other.*]

ROISIN: And what's on the menu tonight?

[BILL *enters.*]

BILL: Good old reliable coq au vin.

ROISIN: What imagination! Ready, Bill?

BILL: Where is Jan tonight, dear?

ROISIN: Good question.

BILL: I don't believe I've set eyes on that lady all day.

ROISIN: Snap.

BILL: With Ronnie, no doubt.

ROISIN: She has been behaving a little strange recently.

BILL: Strange?

ROISIN: Malcolm's rang me the other day. Their new range of jewellery had arrived and she refused to come with me to look it over. Mumbled something about people living on supplementary benefit.

BILL: She what?

ROISIN: Something about supplementary benefit.

BILL: I heard you. What about supplementary benefit?

ROISIN: I didn't quite catch it, but she refused to come with me.

BILL: I wonder what all that's about.

ROISIN: Who knows?

EAMONN: Maybe I was right then.

BILL: About what?

EAMONN: Jan.

ROISIN: What about her?

EAMONN: I was turning into the street yesterday and I saw Jan getting off the bus with a young man. I could have sworn it was the young man from next door.

ROISIN: Ignatius!

EAMONN: I was driving past at the time, but ... I'm sure it was him.

ROISIN: Eamonn, that's the most ridiculous thing ever.

EAMONN: I'm fairly positive.

BILL: Probably just using the same bus.

EAMONN: And holding hands? [ROISIN *laughs aloud.*]

ROISIN: Oh, Eamonn.

EAMONN: I'm not sure you should dismiss it so lightly. I know what I saw. And if it should happen to be true—remember he already has a child. And when a dog has dirtied his box once ...

ROISIN: Eamonn, it's too absurd for words.

BILL: Look here you two. Think of the one place we can escape to tonight where we can forget the McFaddens?

ROISIN [*standing up*]: The Golf Club. [*They exit.*]

SCENE 3

Street. BERNIE *and* JULIA *are inside a brightly-painted Hot Food trailer. They are barely visible behind a cloud of smoke. Hamburgers are cooking on a hot plate.* 'DUFFIN'S HORSE STABLES, PH. C'GEENE 4910' *is written on the trailer.*

BERNIE [*shouting*]: Turn it down!

JULIA: A can't.

BERNIE: Why the hell not?

JULIA: The wee knob's stuck!

[*Both frantically wave the smoke away, coughing and spluttering.*]

BERNIE: Outta m'way and I'll try it. Where is it?

JULIA: Down there! [*We hear the loud hissing of gas.*] Not there! Sufferin' heavens Bernie, d'ya wanna gas is? [*The noise is turned off.*]

BERNIE: What one is it then?

JULIA: Here.

BERNIE: Here?

JULIA: Aye.

BERNIE: Think a got it. That's it.

JULIA: I'm gettin' t'hell outta this.

[*The side door flies open.* JULIA *comes through looking distresed and dishevelled. Her hands are coverd in tomato sauce and a sausage is stuck to her high-heel. She wipes her hands clean and removes the sausage.*]

JULIA: Claire Connery, how are ye?

[BERNIE *joins her, face blackened, paintscraper in hand and holding a bag of prawns.*]

BERNIE: Holy God. A thought you said you worked in Joe Raffo's durin' the war?

JULIA: So a did.

BERNIE: It musta been cleanin' the toilets.

JULIA: B'Jasis, between that smoke and that gas I feel as if a've just come through the Battle of the Somme. And we lost again.

BERNIE: What are w'gonna do? That wee boy'll be back for his four hamburgers. He's the ex-Lord Mayor's son.

JULIA: I don't care if he's one of the starvin' childer of Ethiopa, I'm not goin' back in there, give is a feg—m'throat thinks a'm back workin' in Noble's beg store. [*They light up cigarettes.* BERNIE *goes inside the trailer and returns with two stools. They sit.*]

BERNIE: We were doin' well too.

JULIA: Doin' well? We've probably put Alex outta business.

BERNIE: We sold three-dozen hamburgers and nearly twenty hotdogs. And almost sold one prawn open sandwich.

JULIA: They're not that big a spenders, are the? It's this sort was buyin' margarine long before the rest of is.

BERNIE: Here, did y'see your man Conerney, and his wife, walkin' by?

JULIA: Aye, she's a face that would stop a clock.

BERNIE: And she was old luckin'.

JULIA: Did y'see the state of the poor woman's hair? You'd know it was dyed off her head, wouldn't ye?

BERNIE: Glamour puss? Yid know it was the money was keepin' her together.

JULIA: I always said if I'da had the money, I'd a lucked a million dollars.

BERNIE: As it is, you've only the pension and y'luck more like a crumpled up ten-bob note. [BERNIE *laughs.*] A'm only jokin' love. You're right like, it is the money. Luck at your woman, Roisin. Neither on her nor off her half the time. Covered in make-up from arsehole to breakfast time. Have you noticed her hands? Thon girl hasn't washed a dish in her puff.

JULIA: Sure I know wee Mrs. Crummy that works for her.

BERNIE: Probably gets Mrs. Crummy t'do her ironin' too.

JULIA: And a bet ye she has all the latest gadgets.

BERNIE: I asked Alex to buy me a tumble-dryer and he said, 'Sure we've no tumblers.' But I went out and got one anyway—thought a was in heaven.

JULIA: Not like years ago.

BERNIE: Not a'tall. Many's a time a stud in thon wee scullery of ours doin' a full washin' on a scrubbin' board in the jawbox. Boilin' buckets a water on the stove, do y'mind? A ended up with hands like a dock labourer.

JULIA: A'm sure your woman Roisin has one of them fancy dishwashers.

BERNIE: Oh aye. Y'know, of all the work that's threw on a woman, that's the one thing I've always hated, washin' dishes. Meal after meal after meal, washin' dishes. No end to it.

JULIA: Y'see, there's another one where money comes into it. If you'da had money when you were rearin' your wee family, y'coulda been buyin' disposable plates.

BERNIE: Wouldn't it a been great? 'Dinner over—dishes in the bin!' A was thinkin' a gettin' Alex to buy me one a them microwave ovens.

JULIA: A God, Bernie don't.

BERNIE: Why?

JULIA: Cancer!

BERNIE: Not a'tall. Still, it's nice to have the choice money brings.

JULIA: Oh I don't know. The good things in life brings with them their own problems.

BERNIE: That's true. I was thinkin' the other day about the time I was in havin' my Camillus. The woman facin' me—she was well-t'do—and she was able to tell me that when she went home she would only be seein' her baby for two hours every evenin'. She had a full-time nanny. Did y'ever hear the like of it?

JULIA: I pity them. Luck at that wee girl, Princess Diana. The only time she sees thon wee childer of hers is when the TV cameras comes into Buckingham Palace. You watch. You'd know by the way thon two wee bucks lucks up at her that they're not sure who the hell she is.

BERNIE: And there's thon other one—Fergie. Went d'Australia without her wee chile. I would take the chile off her. Nigh, there is neglect.

JULIA: No social workers runnin' d'her door.

BERNIE: But women like that's bound t'miss out on most of the pleasures of rearin' wee babies.

JULIA: Couldn't be good for the kids either. Sure, it's the childer of the well-t'do that takes all that heroin. Thon Oxford and Cambridge is full a drug addicts. Then the go d'Westminister?

BERNIE: No wonder the country's in the state it's in. All them government ministers got no love when the were wee childer and ended up drug addicts.

JULIA: There's definitely some of the good things in life you're better off without.

BERNIE: I do pity that wee girl, Roisin. Her life's so borin' she has to keep talkin' about her sister in London.

JULIA: If London's so friggin' good, why doesn't she go and live there? London, b'Jasis! Sure who keeps it goin'? The Irish built it, the blacks service it, the Chinese feed it and the American tourists pay for it. The only ones that's like ourselves is the Eastenders.

ALEX [*entering*]: How's it goin', ladies?

JULIA: Oh, here's Colonel Saunders.

ALEX: I sold out.

JULIA: We're bate out.

BERNIE: We done great. W'sold three dozen hamburgers and thirty hot dogs.

JULIA: Then we got fed up and set the hut on fire.

ALEX: I thought a smelt smoke.

BERNIE: We had a wee accident.

JULIA: Bernie spilt a whole container of cookin' oil over the hot plate and we had to abandon ship.

ALEX: Any food destroyed?

JULIA: He's worried about the food. We were nearly burned alive. Y'coulda been sellin' us as chicken nuggets. Alex, I need a wee drop of confidence, run me down to the Rocktown, would ye?

BERNIE: He will not.

ALEX: Sure you're off the drink.

JULIA: Off the drink? Workin' behind there would put ye on LSD!

BERNIE: And you've me on valium.

ALEX: I have a better idea. As soon as we get tidied up here, we're all goin' somewhere special for a drink.

BERNIE: What about that new hotel?

ALEX: You leave it t'me. C'mon til we get cleared up here.

[*They begin to clear up.*]

BERNIE: You'll have to get the lobster soup for tomarra night, Alex. And there was somebody askin' for squid.

ALEX: And who's gonna cook it? Yiz made a pig's arse of doin' simple hamburgers. [*They exit ribbing each other.*]

SCENE 4

JAN *and* IGNATIUS *sitting on the McFadden living-room floor facing each other.*

JAN: Right. [*Reading from a question card*] What did the words 'Open Sesame' actually open?

IGNATIUS: ... A cave.

JAN: Can't accept. It was Ali Baba's cave.

IGNATIUS: Hold on, a said cave, the words Ali Baba—

JAN: But you didn't say 'Ali Baba's cave.'

IGNATIUS: Whadaya want—blood?

JAN: Look, it was you who said answers had to be exactly what it said on the card.

IGNATIUS: Yes, but it's obvious—the answer is, it opened a cave.

JAN: Well, what about my Franco for a piece of pie?

IGNATIUS: But you didn't know his first name.

JAN: And you didn't say Ali Baba. Give me the dice. My turn.

IGNATIUS [*getting up*]: I give up. [*He moves away.*]

JAN [*singing*]: 'Taking the needle. Iggy can't take it.'

IGNATIUS: Shut up.

JAN: All because I was on to my last piece of pie.

IGNATIUS: Wise.

[*Silence as she comes up behind him, puts her arms around his waist and cuddles him.*]

JAN: I've just received word from our producer we can accept 'caves' without the Ali Baba. [*He smiles.*]

IGNATIUS: Bloody Trivial Pursuits. If Alex's hamburgers don't cause a riot in this street, that game will.

JAN: Isn't that what you'd like to see? Riots and disorder on the Bladonmore Road?

IGNATIUS: Love it.

JAN: You've no chance.

IGNATIUS: Has there ever even been a burnin' van strung across this road?

JAN: Nope. I've never even seen an army patrol in our street.

IGNATIUS: No republican marches, loyalist rallies?

JAN: You away in the head?

IGNATIUS: No Union Jacks on the Twelfth, Tricolours at Easter?

JAN: No, Ignatius, wise up.

IGNATIUS: A suppose you've never even seen a riot?

JAN [*thinks for a moment.*]: On the telly.

IGNATIUS: I've started some of the best riots our district ever had. A've one big regret though.

JAN: You're ashamed now of how you behaved?

IGNATIUS: Naa. I'm just ragin' that I was too young for the really big riots in the early 70s. That musta been fantastic. My Uncle Gerry became famous because he was the first rioter to work out how to overcome CS Gas.

JAN: How did he do that?

IGNATIUS: Eight pints of Guinness. It happened by accident, like. One night he left the pub and walked straight into a riot. M'ma says the Brits fired six cannisters of gas and charged. All the lads scattered. But when the gas cleared, the only one still standin'—engaged in hand d'hand combat with 12 Brits—was my Uncle Gerry.

JAN: And what happened to him?

IGNATIUS: Apparently, he put away six Brits

JAN: And then what?

IGNATIUS: By Jasis, my Uncle Gerry could fight.

JAN: But what happened to him?

IGNATIUS: He got his shite knocked in. Got 28 stitches, four cracked ribs, a broken jaw and six months in the Crum. *He* was charged with assault. He's in Purdysburn ever since. When my ma goes up to visit him he's walkin' about with a gas mask on, shoutin', 'Come and get me, Major! Y'know where a am!'

JAN: Speaking of your mother, I wonder how they're getting on with the Bladonmore Road's first squid and hamburger stall.

IGNATIUS: Aye, roll up, roll up, get your squid burgers here!

JAN: Carry-out caviar soup, now on the menu!

IGNATIUS: A bottle a Mundie's wine with every six prawn sandwiches bought! I'd love t'see St. Vincent de Paul Conerney's face when he sees the trailer.

JAN: Not to mention Roisin and Bill.

IGNATIUS: I think I hate Conerney. I hate this whole street.

JAN: But it's not the whole street. The vast majority are reasonable, decent people.

IGNATIUS: They're all full a shit.

JAN: You're full a shit.

IGNATIUS: Jan, it's not right—and I don't care what anybody says— it's not right, that your da can fork out £80,000 for a paintin', while ... while people on the dole are tryin' t'live on thirty or forty pound a week.

JAN: Yes, but you have to accept that the people up here have worked damned hard for their money.

IGNATIUS: It's immoral money.

JAN: Rubbish.

IGNATIUS: What about your man round the corner that hires out the cars?

JAN: What about him?

IGNATIUS: He was caught for turnin' the mileage back on cars he was sellin'. What's hard-earned about that? And know what happened him? He was fined. Do you know that people go to jail in this city for offences involvin' less than £10? And he was fined! They are the sort of people who are banterin' my ma.

JAN: Well, since you've mentioned it, you can't really say that your family hasn't been without fault. [IGNATIUS *is stunned.*] They haven't, Iggy. I mean ... two dogs and a donkey? What about the parties, and now a Hot Food stall, come on Iggy?

IGNATIUS: But you must have the right to buy a house anywhere you want and live in peace.

JAN: That's exactly what I'm saying, Iggy. You're either blind or daft if you can't see that that's what this whole thing is all about. These people bought their houses too and they want to be left in peace. They've lived like this a long time.

IGNATIUS: But they're a shower of stuck-up bleeps.

JAN: In your eyes.

IGNATIUS: Why don't they leave us alone?

JAN: You keep breaking their rules. You keep breaking the most basic standards of behaviour.

IGNATIUS: Their standards. Our standards are different—not lower—different.

JAN: That's a matter of interpretation.

IGNATIUS: Alright, alright. Let's cut across the crap. Even if there was no donkey, no dogs and Camillus was goin' on to be a priest, would my family really be welcome in this street?

JAN: Of course they would. If your mother would ... probably not.

IGNATIUS: Thank you.

JAN: But—

IGNATIUS: But what?

JAN: It can work.

IGNATIUS: How?

JAN: If there's compromise.

IGNATIUS: Compromise, my boolers.

JAN: It can. If the Bladonmore Road behaved a little less precious and your family broke less of their rules—it could work.

IGNATIUS: And we'll all love each other happy ever after and Ba'hai rules okay.

JAN: Don't be so sceptical

IGNATIUS: Jan, let's face facts. This city isn't just divided in two—it's split three ways—Catholics, Protestants and the well-to-do—and that's the real problem.

SCENE 5

Golf Club. ROISIN *is sitting at a table.* BILL *enters with drinks. He sits down.*

BILL: Okay?

ROISIN: Yeah, fine.

BILL: Truce still holding?

ROISIN: That's up to you.

BILL: It was only an innocent remark.

ROISIN: Well, please keep those type of remarks to yourself.

BILL: I didn't mean it. It was a joke.

ROISIN: I didn't see it that way.

BILL: Okay, what did I say? What exactly did I say?

ROISIN: You said I was working-class.

BILL: There, there you see. Paranoia strikes again.

ROISIN: But you did. You said my father was a low-grade civil servant, we lived on the edge of Andersonstown, so I'm working-class. How clever of you, Bill.

BILL: I didn't say that. Look, this whole thing started because I gave off to you for boasting about our proposed trip to Africa.

ROISIN: Boasting?

BILL: I think you were.

ROISIN: I did nothing of the sort.

BILL: You're insecure, Roisin.

ROISIN: You always insist on saying that. I am not insecure about anything.

BILL: Well, I don't feel the need to tell the McFaddens or anyone else every place we've ever been and every ha'penny we've ever spent.

ROISIN: I don't do that.

BILL: I've stood beside you.

ROISIN: Go—and—shite.

BILL: Yes, well, it's hard to argue against that. What did you do to your hair?

ROISIN: Piss off.

BILL: How delightful. You must have been with your father recently.

ROISIN: You wouldn't make a patch for my father's arse.

[EAMONN *enters.*]

BILL: Ah, Eamonn.

EAMONN: Sorry, these 'quick' committee meetings take ages. [BILL *gets up.*]

BILL: What'll you have?

EAMONN: Ah ... gin and tonic please, Bill.

BILL: Coming up. [BILL *exits.*]

EAMONN: Everything all right?

ROISIN: No.

EAMONN: What's the problem?

ROISIN: Him.

EAMONN: What about him?

ROISIN: He's calling me working-class again.

EAMONN [*jokingly*]: He does have a point.

ROISIN: So, you're middle-class and I'm not?

EAMONN: I'm only joking.

ROISIN: Why does everyone 'only joke' with me when they're running me down? And I wish someone would please tell me, what makes a person middle-class?

EAMONN: Toilet rolls.

ROISIN: Eamonn!

EAMONN [*serious*]: Anyone who knew toilet rolls before 1960 is middle-class and anyone who didn't, isn't. Where did you come in?

ROISIN: I need a drink.

EAMONN: Look Roisin, you need that break.

ROISIN: I told you, Eamonn, I can't go.

EAMONN: Why not?

ROISIN: Because that very weekend is Wimbledon Finals. Bill's already bought Centre Court tickets.

EAMONN: Can't you get out of it?

ROISIN: Eamonn, we haven't missed Wimbledon in nine years.

EAMONN: And this is the first time ever that Lynda has decided to go on holiday with her mother.

ROISIN: I'm sorry.

EAMONN: Sorry?

ROISIN: What do you want me to say?

EAMONN: I don't know, I give up.

ROISIN: Look, leave it for now, Eamonn. We can talk after the Legion meeting on Tuesday night, alright?

[BILL *enters with drinks.*]

BILL: What's happening on Tuesday night?

ROISIN: Talking about the McFaddens again.

EAMONN: I was speaking to Inspector Booth.

BILL: Again?

EAMONN: Yes, and he has agreed to act promptly at the next McFadden disturbance.

BILL: Yes, well, I'll tell you something else. I've just been speaking to Ralph and he tells me our 'neighbours' have applied for membership.

ROISIN: Of this Golf Club?

BILL: 'Fraid so.

EAMONN: Of course they have. [*He takes a document out of his inside pocket.*] And this is as far as it goes. [*He slowly tears up the document and drops it in an ashtray.*] What do you think the Committee meeting was about?

[ROISIN *starts laughing.* BILL *joins her. Soon, all three are laughing.*]

ROISIN: Lynda believes we should apply to the World Wildlife Council to have them declared a rare species—that way we can have them caged up! [*More laughter*]

EAMONN: Then they can cook all the hamburgers they want! [*More laughter*]

ROISIN: We're laughing, but they still live next door to me.

BILL: Not to worry. A cuckoo will move into another bird's nest, but it always moves on.

EAMONN: When?

BILL [*pointing*]: Probably not before dinner. Looks like they're going in.

[BILL *drinks up.*]

ROISIN: Yes, let's forget the McFaddens for at least one evening.

BILL: Good idea.

EAMONN [*standing*]: And keep the speech short, Bill old son, if you don't mind. You're not prosecuting any mass murderers tonight.

ROISIN: He's been rehearsing all day.

[*At this* JULIA *enters, carrying a bottle of orange and a glass. She arrives at an empty table across stage from the others. She places her drink on the table, takes her coat off then notices the others.*]

JULIA: Is there anybody sittin' here? [*Silence*] B'Jasis, I feel like a Catholic on his first day at the Shipyard. [*She shouts offstage.*] Bernie! Alex! Over here, there's an empty table over here!

[*The Blakelys and* EAMONN *stare at her in stunned silence.* BERNIE *and* ALEX *enter with drinks.*]

JULIA: Bernie, luck who's here, the leaders of the second Inquisition.

BERNIE: My God, look who it is. King Farouk, Lord Sutch and Lady Muck.

ALEX: I know who they are! They're *The Muppets*!

JULIA: A wonder which one is Miss Piggy. [*They laugh.*]

EAMONN: This Club has a policy of members only.

JULIA: From what I've seen son, the'd take anybody.

ALEX: We were signed in by some friends.

EAMONN. I'll have that checked out.

JULIA: Give yourself a good pull-through with an umbrella, while you're at it.

ROISIN: Mr. McFadden, your son used a swear word to my niece today, right outside my own front door.

JULIA: I told you, Bernie, you shouldn'ta moved up here. The talk of the childer in this street is terrible and your Camillus is gettin' as bad as the rest of them.

BERNIE: I'm just gonna have t'keep him in, so a am, keep him away from them.

ALEX: How do you know Camillus used a swear word?

ROISIN: Because my niece told me. She'd never heard the word before.

ALEX: If she'd never heard it before, how did she know it was a swear word? [ROISIN *is stuck for an explanation.*]

JULIA: I told you, Bernie. Sure, y'couldn't rear a dog in this street. [BILL *stands up.*]

BILL: Let's go outside, Roisin.

[ROISIN *stands. They move to exit.* EAMONN *finishes his drink, stands up and addresses the McFaddens with a smirk on his face.*]

EAMONN: I thought I should inform you, Mr. McFadden. A date has been set for your court appearance in relation to the attack on my wife by your dogs. You'll be receiving the summons any day now. So, see you in court.

ALEX: No problem. See you in court. Oh, and by the way, if yiz aren't doin' anythin' later on, we're havin' a wee bit of a drink in the house, maybe yiz would like to call in?

[*They stare back, then quickly exit.* ALEX *bursts out laughing,* JULIA *and* BERNIE *cheer.*]

BERNIE [*shouting off*]**:** And here! Yiz aren't the only ones that goes t'London we're goin' in September for the World Darts Finals!

ALEX: I said I was goin'.

BERNIE: Plus we're goin' t'Spain for our holidays!

ALEX: We were only luckin' at the brochures, Bernie love.

BERNIE: Yiz aren't the only ones that's been outside Belfast, y'know!

JULIA: And me and her done a lot of travellin' durin' the war, so we did!

BERNIE [*puzzled*]**:** Travelled durin' the war?

JULIA: Smugglin' the butter up from Dundalk, d'ya mind?

BERNIE: Oh aye.

JULIA: The cheek a themens, what? Put a beggar on horseback? [*Shouting*] And I'm takin' up bridge!

ALEX: Imagine. They thought they were chasin' us outta the Bladonmore Road and here we are drinkin' in their Golf Club. Wait'll I tell Big Trevor.

BERNIE: Here, Alex, how did you get us in here?

ALEX: Simple. A walked in with a big bottle of Tamata sauce under m'arm and told the doorman we were the caterers for the dinner. [*They all laugh.*] Immaculate, what?

SCENE 6

The McFadden Home. IGNATIUS *is reading from a book.* JAN *is browsing through Ignatius' record collection. Remnants of catering—sauce bottles, baps, hamburgers, etc. are piled against a wall.*

IGNATIUS: Listen to this, you're a medical student?

JAN: You don't believe everything you read in books, do you?

IGNATIUS: Just listen—

JAN: For heavensake—

IGNATIUS [*reading*]: 'Less less that five per cent of all medical students at university come from working-class backgrounds. This does not mean that the working-classes are less intelligent, only that very few would see themselves as potential members of a professional class. Their environment—both at home and in the school—does not encourage them to think that they could become doctors ... '

JAN: Look, I haven't said that's not true.

IGNATIUS: Also ... [*Reading*] 'A child from a middle-class background has a twenty times better chance of going to university than a working-class child.' All this, Jan, is determined before the child leaves the mother's womb. And you say class division is exaggerated?

JAN: What are you promoting here—class war? Are we talking about the failed system of communism?

IGNATIUS: Not a'tall. We're talkin' about the here and now. About what exactly is outside that front door. We're talkin' Helen's Bay and Divis Flats, we're talkin' Cultra and Sandy Row, Malone

Road and Falls Road. The failure of Soviet communism doesn't obliterate those divisions.

JAN: Quite finished, Iggy Marx?

IGNATIUS [*tittering*]: This last bit's funny.

JAN: Ah no ...

IGNATIUS: 'Working-class mothers may hinder their child's development, since they do not spend as much time as middle-class mothers in talking to their children, nor do they give such constructive answers to their questions.' He's spot on there. I remember my ma. [*Mimics*]

'No!', 'Shut your bake!', 'None a your business!', 'Away and lick m'arse!' No doubt about it. The most important division in the world is the class division.

JAN: I don't believe in any divisions—people are people.

IGNATIUS: Well, when you come across a barrister marryin' a shop assistant, let me know.

JAN: I'm sure it has happened.

IGNATIUS: It can't. They would never meet. The middle-class have their social circles and the workin'-class have theirs.

JAN: Don't exaggerate.

IGNATIUS: I'm not.

JAN: Rubbish. That means there is no such thing as love. And certainly no such thing as love at first sight.

IGNATIUS: How do you work that out?

JAN: Because, I mean, if a girl from a wealthy background sees a boy—anywhere—and is instantly attracted to him, maybe he is stunningly handsome with the most gorgeous eyes—what you are saying is that if he was a binman, the attraction would end immediately?

IGNATIUS: Immediately? If he was a binman—and he as much as winked at her—she'd have him arrested!

JAN: Rubbish.

IGNATIUS: Jan, love might be a powerful thing—but it does not transcend class borders.

JAN: Do you know what *I* think?

IGNATIUS: Tell me.

JAN: I think you're afraid.

IGNATIUS: Of what?

JAN: Of everything I am. You're afraid to admit to yourself that you're in love with a nice, middle-class girl.

IGNATIUS: Where's your brain.

JAN: The very thought terrifies you, I know it does. Iggy, I want you
   to think of us as people. No labels, no badges, just people. Our
   feelings for each other. [IGNATIUS *remains silent, thoughtful.*] Do
   you believe in love?

IGNATIUS: That's a big one.

JAN: Do you?

IGNATIUS: Can I confer?

JAN: Answer the question.

IGNATIUS: Do I believe in love? Yes ... and no. What I mean is ... Love
   is like religion, you'll find it if you need it.

JAN: Are you looking?

IGNATIUS: Are you?

JAN: Yes. And you?

IGNATIUS: Naa, not really. But I met this middle-class hure from the
   Bladonmore Road recently who's studyin' medicine at—
   [*They punch each other playfully and then kiss.*]

JAN: Do you think our parents would accept it?

IGNATIUS: Accept what?

JAN: If we told them we were going to get married?

IGNATIUS: Ah nigh, hold on a minute—

JAN: I love you, Iggy.

IGNATIUS: Tell me more.

JAN: I want to be with you every minute of the day.

IGNATIUS: Even if I need to go to the toilet sometimes?

JAN: I'll wait outside.

IGNATIUS: Will you explain to my ma that the kids will be brought
   up Ba'hai?

JAN: I might have to.

IGNATIUS: Come again?

JAN: My period was due a week ago.
   [IGNATIUS *is speechless.* JAN *puts on music, Sam Cooke singing* 'You
   Send Me'.]

IGNATIUS: A'm only 22. And I'm an unmarried father of two.

JAN: Come on, let's dance. [*They dance.*] I only said it was a week overdue.

IGNATIUS: They say a week is a long time in politics. Two minutes
   can be a lifetime in sex.
   [JULIA *enters downstage, singing.*]

JULIA: 'If I said you had a beautiful body
   Would you houl' it fernenst me.
   If I said you were a devil
   Wud ya trate me like an angel the night ...'

[JULIA *enters the house, still singing and dancing and giving a few shakes of the hips in an attempt to be sexy.*]

IGNATIUS: Hamburgers all sold, Julya?

JULIA: Fla you and your hamburgers—who's doin' barman?

IGNATIUS: I thought you were off the drink?

JULIA: Ach, a got fed up. Says I d'myself, 'Julya, who are y'stayin' sober for?' I woke up this mornin' and didn't know whether I felt like a bear with a sore arse or a prize cow bein' artificially inseminated. Y'need the confidence, y'need the confidence. Sixty-six years is a hell of a long wait.

[BERNIE *and* ALEX *enter.* ALEX *is inebriated.*]

ALEX: Do you disagree?

BERNIE: No, y'done right, y'done right to tell him to take himself off, y'done right.

ALEX: Bernie, did I do right? Like, be honest nigh, did I do the right thing or not?

BERNIE: Yes, y'did exactly the right thing, love. Y'did the only thing any man would do.

ALEX: Are y'sure?

[BERNIE *stops at the rhododendron.*]

BERNIE: Did y'hear about m'rhodydendren?

ALEX: No, what?

BERNIE: Died on me.

ALEX: Hyre?

BERNIE: I wished a knew.

[*They enter the house.*]

BERNIE: Ignatius, how did you say the rhodydendren died?

IGNATIUS: Dunno. Musta been too much lime in the soil. Rhodies don't like lime. Hey Alex, you're drunk.

ALEX: Wisht a was. Alright, Jan love?

JAN: Fine, Alex.

ALEX: Iggy, get some drinks.

BERNIE: The baby asleep?

IGNATIUS: Yes. But I had t'change a big dirty nappy.

JAN: He did not. I changed it and the child has slept all night, Mrs. McFadden.

ALEX: Where's the Camillus fella?

IGNATIUS: Bed. But he's covered in white paint.

ALEX: White paint?

IGNATIUS: I caught him out the back painting the donkey's legs with white emulsion. He said he wanted to be able to ride it at night.

BERNIE: I'll swing for that wee lad, so a will, swing for him.

[IGNATIUS*and* JAN *are dishing out the drinks.* JULIA *is holding up a glass as* JAN *pours, then stops.*]

JAN: That enough?

JULIA: What way were you reared, love?

JAN: You want some more?

JULIA: Want more? By the end of this night love, I want the confidence to be oooooozzzzin' outta me. Nigh, a didn't mean any harm t'you, Jan love, do y'know what a mean? [*They smile at each other but* JULIA *suddenly snaps the bottle from* JAN *and resumes smiling.*] No harm love, but it'll save your wee feet.

[JAN *smiles, embarrassed.*]

ALEX: Take a drink, love, and sit down and take no heed of that oul' doll. Right, everybody got a drink? Cause my wife ... we're celebratin' tonight cause my wife ... my honeybee, Bernie, passed her driving test ... after a hundred and two lessons! [*They all cheer or jeer.*]... and eleven attempts! [*More cheering and jeering*] So. A'd like yiz all to drink t'my wife, Bernie, and may she have many happy hours on the road—like a mean, the *car* on the road, her inside it—[*Cheering*]—no, all jokin' aside, a'd like yiz all t'drink to Bernie for passin' her test, and to ... ourselves.

JULIA: Here, here!

[*They all drink. The phone rings.*]

ALEX: I'll get it. [*Lifts receiver*] Hello. That's right. And who are you? One of my neighbours? Noise? We live in the street too, y'know. Will ye? Is that right? Well, y'know what you can do, don't ye? Fuck off! [*He slams the phone down.*]

BERNIE: Who was that?

ALEX: Somebody luckin' to come to the party.

JULIA: Let them run on.

ALEX: I know a good idea. Big Trevor and themens—[*Looks at watch*]—will be just gettin' threw out of the Engineers b'nigh, they'll be bustin' for a drink. [*Starts dialing*]

JULIA: Get him t'bring up some Carlsberg Specials.

[IGNATIUS *pours* BERNIE *a drink.*]

BERNIE: Ignatius, son ...

IGNATIUS: What?

BERNIE: Do you think George Orwell was right in the head?

IGNATIUS: Ah ma, not more 'O' Level stuff.

BERNIE: But do ye?

IGNATIUS: 'Course he was.

BERNIE: Then why, why did he—nigh answer me this—why did he write a book about sheep and pigs and horses ... and forget to tell everybody that it was a children's book?

IGNATIUS: It's not a children's book. It's about Russia.

BERNIE: Somebody mentioned that, but I've searched that book from cover to cover and Russia's not mentioned once.

[ALEX *finishes on the phone.*]

ALEX: Big Trevor and the lads—on their way up! [*Cheers*]

JULIA: Here, here! Ring the Rocktown and get Mickey Kelly up!

BERNIE: Aye, get Mickey up. Y'always get a song outta Mickey.

JULIA: Luckin' terrible well he is, luckin' terrible well.

BERNIE: Go on, Alex, ring the Rocktown and get some of them up. Sarah Jane McCartney and Maisie Baker and themens. We'll have a geg.

JULIA: All our oul' chums.

ALEX: You ring, Bernie love.

BERNIE: I'll ring then.

[BERNIE *starts dialing.* IGNATIUS *pours* ALEX *a drink.*]

IGNATIUS: We were just talkin' there, Alex, me and Jan.

ALEX: Aye, what were yiz wafflin' about?

IGNATIUS: We were just tryin' to work out whether a hamburger has a sex life or not?

ALEX: In the name a fffffuu ...

IGNATIUS: 'M'only jokin'. We were talkin' about the rich and the poor, know the way you're a capitalist ...?

ALEX: I'm not a capitalist!

IGNATIUS: You are!

ALEX: Jesis Christ, Ignatius son, I'm up t'here in debt.

IGNATIUS: Yes, but do you consider yourself middle-class now that you live on the Bladonmore Road?

ALEX: Me! Middle-class! For a start a'm not even sure what it is but a know a don't sound like no Hooray Henry. And we're just outta that Golf Club. Do you think I would sit among—[*To* JAN] no harm to you, love—among thon shower of assholes? No way. Ignatius son, y'don't have t'live among monkeys to enjoy a banana. I only moved up here because your ma, that—[*Pointing to* BERNIE]—carried-away, grandeur-lovin' eejit of an oul' ...

[BERNIE *puts the phone down and abruptly turns around.*]

Get your ma a wee drink, would ye?

JULIA: Any a them comin', Bernie?

BERNIE: A was talkin' t'Mickey Kelly.

JULIA: Were y'talkin' t'Mickey?

BERNIE: He has his son with him. His son's drivin' an Education and Library Board mini-bus.

JULIA: And are the comin' up?

BERNIE: The whole bar's comin' up! [*They all cheer.*] An Education and Library Board mini-bus?

JULIA: That'll be Mickey's big son, Joe.

BERNIE: Didn't he used t'drive for the Hospital?

JULIA: Aye, but he was caught drunk-drivin' an ambulance on the Gov'ner Road. He had the sirens on and everything—said he was tryin t'catch the Rock Bar afore closin' time. He got six months.

ALEX: Right, Bernie love, a wee song?

JULIA: Yes, Bernie, the very thing.

ALEX: Give is ... our song?

JULIA: Would y'listen to that? [JULIA *speak to* IGNATIUS *and* JAN.] Bridget Wilson was askin' me how them two was gettin' on—I see Bridget every week when a'm collectin' m'pension—I says, I told her, 'They're as happy as pigs in shit.' Says I, 'Bridget. Alex McFadden loves our Bernie more than Douglas Fairbanks loved Mary Pickford.'

[BERNIE *starts singing quietly*, 'My Foolish Heart'. *Not long into it she is interrupted by the loud, constant ringing of the doorbell.*]

ALEX: That'll be Big Trevor and the lads.

IGNATIUS: I'll get it.

JULIA: Carry on, Bernie.

[EAMONN CONERNEY *enters aggressively.*]

EAMONN: I've had to leave the Golf Club.

ALEX: What, thrown out for vomitin' on the carpet?

EAMONN: My wife has had 12 different callers to the house tonight.

JULIA: I told yiz what sorta district this was.

EAMONN: Mr. McFadden, as Secretary of the Association and on behalf of all residents, I am formally requesting you to immediately put an end to the noise emanating from this house.

ALEX: What noise?

EAMONN: We have had enough.

BERNIE: So have we.

EAMONN: The Residents' Association—

ALEX [*standing beside him*]: You've made your request—nigh beat it!

EAMONN: I'll have to call in the police.

JULIA: Y'can call in the Gurka Rifles for all the hell we care.

BERNIE: Away and leave us alone!

EAMONN: This is your last warning. I'm going straight to the police.

[EAMONN *turns to exit*]

JULIA: Good. Y'can take this with you!

[JULIA *throws a pile of uncooked sausages at* EAMONN. *He ducks and exits under a shower of hamburgers, sausages, baps etc.* ALEX *closes the door behind him. The phone rings.* ALEX *answers it.*]

ALEX: Yes. That's right. No. Yes. Fuck you too.

IGNATIUS: Who was that?

ALEX: The ex-Lord Mayor. Right, Ignatius, let's have some music, kid.

IGNATIUS: No problem.

ALEX: What are y'puttin' on?

JAN: One guess?

ALEX: Sam friggin' Cooke. [*Instantly, we hear Sam Cooke,* 'Twisting The Night Away', *at high volume. They all get up and twist. After a moment the phone rings.* ALEX *answers. He immediately turns around and gestures for* IGNATIUS *to turn the music off. This happens.*] Yes, Inspector. [*To others*] It's the cops! That's right, Inspector. McFadden. Alex McFadden. Number 31. I'm afraid you must have the wrong house, Inspector. As a matter of fact we've just had a death in the family. Hmm. That's right. The wife's sister, Julia. Oh, it was very sudden, heart attack. Monday mornin' Inspector, after ten a'clock mass. Not a'tall. And yourself. Bye.

[ALEX *puts the phone down.*]

JULIA: Y'dirty cowbeg ye!

ALEX: A had d'say something. C'mon you anyway, it's your turn for an oul' number.

BERNIE: Yes Julya, come on, I sung.

JULIA: I'm not singin'.

IGNATIUS: Come on, Aunt Julya.

JULIA: The only time I sing is when a'm comin' or goin' somewhere. When a'm there, a'm too busy drinkin'.

IGNATIUS: Jan sings.

JAN: I do not!

IGNATIUS: She knows a whole lotta Ba'hai songs.

BERNIE: Aye, a good oul' Ba'hai.

ALEX: Right Jan, one song.

JULIA: That's a girl.

IGNATIUS: Can't refuse now.

JAN [*slapping him*]: See you.

ALEX: Quiet nigh.

[JAN *sings* 'Love Letters'. *Halfway through the doorbell is rung, furiously.*]

ALEX: Keep on singing. [ALEX *goes to the window and looks out.*] It's your man Eamonn again. Ignatius, get me the fire extinguisher. [IGNATIUS *exits.*] Keep singing, Jan.

[*The doorbell rings continously.* JAN *continues singing.* JULIA *stocks up with hamburgers etc.* IGNATIUS *returns with fire extinguisher.* ALEX *takes it and shoots at Eamonn through the letter-box. We hear his shouting and swearing as he runs off.* ALEX *moves into the middle of the room and conducts the 'Choir' on the last lines of* 'Love Letters'. *They all applaud.*]

ALEX: Immaculate, Jan love, well done.

JAN: Can I say something? I love the way you can all sit around and sing. [*They all stare quizzically, in silence.*] I mean, I've never seen anything like this before.

BERNIE: But youse have parties.

JAN: Yeah, but ... but they're usually stand-up affairs and all that happens is that boring people stand around talking ... and talking and talking—that's it—then home.

JULIA: Well, if y'didn't sing when y'got rightly, what else is there t'do? Some of the best nights of my life, a had, singin' m'head off after a few drinks. Oh aye, very good for ye, better than any prescription a doctor could give ye.

BERNIE: Alex, ring the Rocktown and see what's keepin' themens.

[BERNIE *and* ALEX *go to the phone.* IGNATIUS *looks depressed.* JAN *puts a comforting arm around him.*]

JULIA: Is there something wrong between youse two?

IGNATIUS: Yeah, I wanna shoot her da and she won't let me.

JAN: It's him. He has a hang-up because of my background.

JULIA: Ignatius son, you're bein' very petty about this. If Jan was to marry you, have a couple of wee childer, mix a wee bit more with ordinary people and learn how to speak with a proper Belfast accent, who knows, it mightn't be long before she was normal just like the rest of us.

[JAN *is dumbfounded.* ALEX *and* BERNIE *come off the phone.*]

BERNIE: Julya, the mini-bus has left and they're all on their way up! [*Cheers*]

JULIA: Stickin' out.

[*The doorbell rings again.* IGNATIUS *checks.*]

IGNATIUS: It's your man Eamonn back—with Mr. and Mrs. Blakely. [*Moving to the fire extinguisher*] The fire extinguisher!

ALEX: No, let them in.

JAN: Mr. McFadden, don't open the door—please.

ALEX: Sorry, love. We have to get this over with, once and for all.

[*He nods to* IGNATIUS *to open the door. They enter.*]

ROISIN [*furious, pointing at* JAN]: Home! [*No response*] I said, home!

JAN: No.

ROISIN: What do you mean no, Jan Blakely? I insist on you leaving this house this instant.

JAN: I'm not going.

BILL: Why don't you come home and talk to us about it, dear?

ROISIN: She's done it now. She has done it now, Bill. I'm not having her back in my house.

BILL: Take it easy, Roisin.

ROISIN: But what is she doing here among among these people? Among other things, Bill, there's a child in this house, born out of wedlock.

BERNIE: Who the hell do you think you're talkin' about?

JULIA: There's no wife-swappers among us!

ROISIN: I don't know what you're alluding to, but I should inform you that it's now perfectly clear to the residents of this road, that the general conduct of this family does not meet the required standards for residing here.

BERNIE: Standards? What standards?

EAMONN: Ordinary, decent, civilised standards.

ALEX: What would you know about standards?

EAMONN: Anything I would say I'm sure would be lost.

ALEX: Is that right? Well, I run a wee business m'self but a would never build a house knowin' it would start fallin' down five years later.

EAMONN: What are you referring to?

ALEX: T'you—O.P. Conerney the Builders. From building sub-standard tower blocks that are being knocked down this very minute to cross-border smugglin', to pillars of the Catholic Church, I know all about O.P. Conerney the Builders.

EAMONN: What you have just said, I should warn you, is extremely libellous.

ALEX: And what are y'gonna' do? Call in your legal representative, William Blakely, solicitor? Currently owns 51 per cent of Downtown Amusements, suppliers of gambling machines to half the backstreet clubs in Belfast?

ROISIN: Bill, are you going to take this?

BILL: We're really wasting our time here, Roisin. Let's go.

EAMONN: I've never heard so much drivel.

ALEX: Well, if it's drivel, you take me to court.

EAMONN: I fully intend to.

ALEX: Good. Trevor McCrudden will be my main witness.

EAMONN: Who?

ALEX: You remember Big Trevor? He was your general foreman for years, then he went on to work as a heavy for Downtown Amusements—on your recommendation, as you will no doubt recall, Eamonn.

EAMONN: I haven't a notion what you're talking about.

ALEX: I know you do.

EAMONN: Mr. McFadden, among other things, you are a liar.

ALEX: Sorry?

EAMONN: A liar. And the sooner you leave here, the better. They are building some quite good itinerant sites.

JULIA: The bastard.

BERNIE: What did he say?

ALEX [*striding forward*]: Right. [*Pointing angrily at* EAMONN] You! Me and you outside.

[ALEX *grabs* EAMONN *by the lapels.* IGNATIUS *steps forward to support* ALEX, BERNIE *goes to restrain him.*]

BILL: Really, Mr. McFadden.

ALEX [*pointing in Bill's face*]: Fuck up you, or I'll hit you too.

ROISIN: I told you we should have brought the police with us.

BERNIE: C'mon Alex, leave it, let them run on.

ALEX: C'mon you! Outside and we'll sort this out.

BERNIE: Alex!

ALEX: Sorry Bernie, but this joker has tortured us since we moved in here—I'm havin' no more of it. [*He shakes* EAMONN.] I'm gonna kill this guy. Fair go, me and you.

EAMONN: So typical, really. Every dispute must be settled with the methods of the backstreets.

ALEX: Well, youse hold all the other cards—this is the only one I can play.

ROISIN: C'mon, Eamonn. We'll let the police deal with these people.

JULIA: If you don't get out love, I'll deal with you.

BILL: Let's go darling.

[BILL *ushers* ROISIN *to the door.*]

ROISIN: I'm going. But I'm warning you. If my child is not—

JAN: I am not a child!

ROISIN: —If she is not home within an hour—I will be asking the police to proceed with kidnapping charges.

[*At this* JULIA *throws a handful of hamburgers at* ROISIN.]

JULIA: Here, kidnap these!

[JULIA *throws more meat, as the* BLAKELYS *and* EAMONN CONERNEY *exit.* JULIA *pursues them to the door. She closes the door.*]

IGNATIUS: Julya.

JULIA: What?

IGNATIUS: You've just cost Alex about three nights' profit.

JULIA: It was worth every penny!

[*The phone rings.* ALEX *answers.* BERNIE, *deep in thought, sits down.*]

ALEX: Yes? No. [*He slams the phone down. The phone rings again.*] Yes? Trevor! Where the hell are ye? Lost? 31 Bladonmore Road. You'll see the peelers outside it. [IGNATIUS *is repelling the intruders at the front door.* ALEX *puts the phone down. It rings instantly. He answers.*] Yes. Two dogs and a donkey? Where? Your front lawn? Y'wouldn't be able to give them a feed by any chance, and put them down for the night?

[*He puts the phone down. At this* JAN *notices that* BERNIE *is crying. She nods to* ALEX, *who immediately goes to her side.*]

ALEX: What's wrong, Bernie? [*The others stop what they are doing and look at* BERNIE.] Bernie, what is it love?

BERNIE [*fighting tears*]**:** Nothin', nothin'.

ALEX: C'mon nigh, Bernie, there's no need for this. Come on. What is it love? Tell me.

[BERNIE *regains some control. She looks up and stares straight ahead.*]

BERNIE: A wanna go home.

ALEX: What?

BERNIE: A wanna go home, Alex.

ALEX: This is your home.

BERNIE: It's not.

ALEX: Of course it is. We worked hard t'get here. This is our house.

BERNIE: Them people's right. I don't belong here. A wanna go back to the docks.

ALEX: Don't be silly.

BERNIE: A'm not bein' silly. This was all a mistake. A terrible mistake. I'm sorry, Alex, for askin' you t'come up here. A shoulda knew, but a thought a was doin' it for the best, t'give Ignatius and Antionette a better chance in life. And wee Julie Lorenzia, a wanted her t'not even know what we came through. And a wanted Camillus to go to a new school, new chums. A didn't know he would come home cryin' cause one of his schoolmasters made fun of the way he talked. And a miss my Antionette terrible terrible. And on top of all that, a miss our way. A really do miss the oul' district, the neighbours. There's wee Mrs. Ferran—I used t'collect her pension for her every Tuesday and run her messages, cause she wasn't able t'get out. A haven't seen nor heard of her since we left. A haven't seen any of m'oul' neighbours since w'left. Do you know what I was tryin' t'do? I was tryin' to forget them. A was tryin' t'put them outta m'mind. A was denyin' everything a ever was—to m'self. I thought this place woulda been so different. Shalamar? Maybe it all came too late in life for me. Then again, in the shape a things, maybe a wasn't meant for it. A thought that anyway, when a saw the rhodydendron dead. I wanna go home, Alex.

ALEX: You're upset love, we'll talk about it later.

BERNIE: No, Alex, it's not just tonight and the way these people have behaved, I've been thinkin' hard about it—and a wanna go back home.

ALEX: But that would be givin' in. *We* are letting *them* intimidate us! Think about it—intimidate us! We have as much right as anybody to live here.

BERNIE: But they don't—

ALEX [*flaring up*]: Fuck them! Fuck them! They will not intimidate me. It's no great odds t'me that their houses is comin' down with £80,000 paintings, I couldn't giva monkey's shit about their weekends in Paris and London and their specially imported boxes of wine. Fuck them! Okay, the speak polite and play golf. Well, I like my life too. I'm not movin'.

IGNATIUS: I agree that we shouldn't be intimidated by them but I also think we should move.

ALEX: Shit!

IGNATIUS: Alex, there's plenty of other places t'live. We don't have to put up with this. How could we deal with these people after all that's happened? It's alright for you, you'll be out workin' most of the time but m'ma has t'be here all day, every day. I say, sit tight for the minute—but move when it suits us.

ALEX: I'm not goin' anywhere.

BERNIE: Well, I am.

IGNATIUS: We would never get peace in this street no matter what happens.

JULIA: I don't know why yiz are fightin' nigh. I coulda told yiz this would happen from the day and hour a walked inta this street. These people sees themselves as rare birds and they've spent years buildin' up a good nest. They don't want a family of street-pigeons landin' down on top of them.

BERNIE: Is that the way you see us?

JULIA: You're not listenin'. A said that's the way *they* see *us*. And it's always been like that—from I was a chile anyway. Did y'ever see a big nest? No. Nests are small, there's always only room for a few. Ignatius son, give is a wee glass a confidence.

ALEX: Aye, let's all have a drink. We're still celebratin', remember? Big Trevor and the lads'll be here any minute. Wanna drink, Bernie?

BERNIE [*pauses*]: Certainly, why not?

ALEX: That's what I like to hear. When my honeybee's happy, I'm happy.

JULIA: Hey Bernie, d'ya mind the time me and you went out with the two Dutch Sailors?

BERNIE: The couldn't speak a word of English between them.

JULIA: Aye, but the knew what their hands was for.

BERNIE: The one you were with said he was the ship's cook.

JULIA: Aye, he kneaded my breasts like the were dough for an applecake.

BERNIE: The one I was with wouldn't spend a ha'penny. Kept showin' me how much money he had, but wouldn't spend a ha'penny. A musta walked him up and down past the clothes shops in Royal Avenue ten times, but all he wanted to do was go to the pub.

JULIA: Why did I always have the bad luck? I always fell in with teetotallers, chapel men and born-again Christians. I'da give anything to be swept aff m'feet by a no-good, layabout alcoholic. [*The phone rings.*] Let me answer that. [*Grabs the phone. Singing*] 'If you knew Susie like I knew Susie
Oh, oh whatta gal ... '
[ALEX *takes the phone off her and replaces it. It rings again. He lifts the phone and throws it in a bin.*]

ALEX: The neighbours is complain' again. So let's give them something to complain about. Ignatius, music!

IGNATIUS: Comin' up. [*The phone can be heard ringing inside the bin.*]

BERNIE: Something we can dance to, Ignatius. C'mon Julya, I wanna dance.
[IGNATIUS *plays the Conga. Everyone gets up and dances. Then* ALEX *leads them in single file around the living-room. He takes the fire extinguisher with him, letting go a blast from it every now and again.*]

ALEX [*shouting*]: Okay everybody, out! We're gonna dance on the Bladonmore Road.

[*They cheer and dance across downstage.*]

JULIA: Wait, wait, wait, stop! Stop! [*They stop.*] I have an announcement to make.

IGNATIUS: What, you're pregnant?

JULIA: A'm gettin' married! [*Cheers*]

ALEX: Who to?

JULIA: Do y'know Ralph next door?

BERNIE: What about him?

JULIA: Well, he asked me to marry him.

BERNIE: Get away d'hell's gates a'that w'ye.

JULIA: He did. But after searchin' for 66 years I've finally decided a'm gonna marry Mickey Kelly! [*Cheers*]

ALEX: Hey waita minute. I was talkin' to Mickey yesterday and he never mentioned anything.

JULIA: Oh, Mickey doesn't know. I haven't told him yet.

[*The music resumes louder. They dance across stage and off.*]

Black-out